BRITISH COLUMBIA
Shipwrecks

T.W. Paterson

STAGECOACH PUBLISHING CO. LTD.
P.O. Box 3399, Langley, B.C. V3A 4R7

Typesetting, layout and design by
Stagecoach Publishing Co. Ltd.

Printed in Canada by
D.W. Friesen & Sons Ltd.

First Printing—October 1976

Canadian Cataloguing in Publication Data

Paterson, Thomas W., 1943-
   British Columbia shipwrecks

   Includes bibliography and index.
   ISBN 0-88983-005-3
   ISBN 0-88983-007-X pa.

   1. Shipwreck - British Columbia.
2. British Columbia - History. I. Title.
FC3820.S5P38   917.11   C76-016050-3
F1088.P

Introduction

Storm, hidden reef, primitive navigation, human error and Indian attack have accounted for hundreds of vessels, and thousands of lives, during the past 200 years; making shipwreck one of the greatest threats to life and limb in British Columbia history.

Even today, with the latest in electronic warning gear, and navigation by satellite, this hazard remains, and few mariners have forgotten that one jagged stretch of Vancouver Island was once dreaded world-wide as being the Graveyard of the Pacific.

Renewed attention has been focussed upon the dangers of these shores, British Columbians watching with growing concern as the day nears when mammoth tankers forge a seagoing pipeline between Alaskan oil fields and Washington refineries. Environmentalists accept future shipwrecks as being inevitable—with all of their horrors for beaches and wildlife on both sides of the 49th parallel.

One can only hope that such a catastrophe will be avoided. But a look at the record, even of recent years, is far from reassuring...

Author's Notes

The author takes this opportunity to "apologize" to readers for the recurring mention of Victoria and that city's oldest newspaper, the *Daily Colonist*. In choosing which maritime disasters to depict here, it became evident that both city and newspaper were being cited time and time again; at the risk, perhaps, of alienating those readers from other parts of the province who may feel that the author is guilty of parochialism.

It simply was a question of going with the record. For Victoria was the marine, as well as provincial capital of British Columbia until surpassed in the former capacity by Vancouver. As for the *Colonist*, this historic journal, as well as being the oldest newspaper in the province, is a faithful chronicle of the province's maritime heritage.

Hopefully, readers will forgive what might seem over-emphasis of both and accept *British Columbia Shipwrecks* as one writer's attempt to show what it was really like to "go down to the sea in ships" in days gone by.

T.W. PATERSON

Chapter 1

Mystery Wrecks

British Columbia waters have exacted a heavy toll of life and property since the day wooden ships and iron men first defied storm and reef to explore, then exploit, her forbidding shores, and today grim reminders of these forgotten tragedies are still to be seen on windswept beach and in eerie depth by beachcomber and skindiver.

But the sea guards her secrets well, and too often these skeletons of once-proud windjammer and steamship defeat all attempts at identification, even when the miracle tools of the 20th century are employed. And so "mystery wrecks" they remain.

Many reports of disaster at sea have been recorded over the past century, settlers, Indians and passing ships bringing word of wreckage washed upon a remote beach, the sighting of a smashed, empty lifeboat, a listing hulk hailed without answer.

One of the first, and most intriguing, of these unsolved puzzles is that of Long Beach's "Spanish galleon." How long the bones of this unknown wooden ship have rested here, deep in the famous white sands at the western end of the beach, is not known, although the first whites to settle at Tofino heard tales of the mystery wreck from older Indians of the region.

The natives could tell nothing of the landlocked corpse beyond the fact it had been there before their lifetime, which would suggest it to be at least 150-years-old. Who was she? How did she die? Where was she from?

Today few know her exact location, just above the high-water line, and but 100 feet from the highway. According to George Nicholson, in *Vancouver Island's West Coast,* driftwood, scrub spruce and beach weeds now cover the site.

"Shortly before the First Great War," he writes, "a group of American university students spent a summer investigating the wreck, but the only tools they had to work with were picks and shovels. They did, however, manage to expose the upper part of the hull, but heavy seas which coincided with a high spring tide buried it again, and as their time was limited they were forced to abandon the project. The students took back with them, for further study, photographs, measurements, specimens of timbers, spikes and copper fastenings, but whether the vessel or its country of origin has since been identified is not known."

Some years ago inquiries were made of several northwestern universities and museums as to whether their files contained references to Long Beach's long lost "galleon," but without success. One promising lead, the University of Minnesota, had yielded a similar result. From 1901-07, the Minnesota Seaside Station had operated at Botanical Beach, near Port Renfrew. However, despite the fact "the activities of this enterprise are quite thoroughly documented," the university could find no mention of a summer spent by its students in unearthing a mystery ship.

Many years have passed since the unknown expedition's gallant attempt, and the wreck lies there yet, disturbed only by the occassional treasure hunter who has learned of its location from the few knowledgeable pioneers still living. Unfortunately, it would involve a major undertaking — or a bulldozer — in excavating it completely.

The remains of other ill-fated vessels can be seen along the moody west coast from time to time, uncovered briefly by storm. Here and there streaks of rust reveal the forgotten resting place of ancient wreckage. The British barque *Mustang* died on Long Beach a century ago; periodically, the enormous anchor and broken links of her chain are exposed by wind and tide, only to be hidden once more, after reminding visitors that once Vancouver Island's jagged western shores were feared the world over by the hardy seafarers of a vanished age.

Perhaps B.C.'s best known mystery wreck is that of lonely Sydney Inlet, Clayoquot Sound, where, in 1958, an American expedition located the wreckage of an ancient ship. Dr. George Cottrell, of Portland, and his party had been in search of the legendary *Tonquin*, sunk during an Indian attack, when they found the hulk.

Upon discovering it could not be that of *Tonquin*, the adventurers had interested the Royal Canadian Navy in investigating and identifying the wreck. That October, the naval auxiliary vessel *Laymore* visited the site with members of the RCN diving school, joining the minesweeper HMCS *James Bay*, then on exercises in the area.

Relocating the wreck in a bay at the northern side of the inlet, navy divers reported her bow to be in six fathoms, while her stern sheered downward to a depth of 12 fathoms. One problem encountered by divers was that the wreckage was scattered about the murky seabed, and buried in sand, mud and rock. Despite this, they were able to estimate the ship's dimensions as having been approximately 150 feet long, with a beam of 35 feet.

Using the minesweeper's lifting gear, divers recovered a comprehensive inventory of relics, some of which are presently on display in the B.C. Maritime Museum, Victoria. "They included," states a navy report, "a 62-foot Phillipine (mahogany) mast, an ancient anchor measuring eight feet in length, a 12-foot-long, hand-worked windlass, a great capstan of teak wood to which were attached broken lengths of very wide (17½ inches wide and six inches thick) teakwood planking, and the ship's bilge pump, made a cast iron, in which the leather valves were still visible.

"Underneath the copper sheathing the wood is in a remarkable state of preservation. Elsewhere on the winch, time, marine life and the action of the sea have left their mark."

One of the more curious observations had been a large number of rotted, hollow logs strewn about the wreckage, and originally thought to be the remains of a long-ago attempt at salvage by strapping bundles of logs about the hulk.

Further investigation led to the conclusion that the logs, shaped by axe and saw to fit the ship's hold, had made up its cargo, which conformed with records; timber and salmon had formed a lucrative trade between Vancouver Island and the Sandwich (Hawaiian) Islands.

Another source of endless conjecture is the fact wood recovered from the wreck is charred. Had, like tragic *Tonquin*, the mystery ship been attacked by Indians, or was she victim of disaster on the high seas, and had drifted, a blackened hulk, to her final berth in Sydney Inlet's brooding depths?

Historians were intrigued by a copper penny which scientists dated as having been minted between 1839-60.

In a last attempt at identification, navy divers returned to Sydney Inlet, in January, 1962, to search for a silver nail thought to be imbedded in the stern at the point where it joins the keel. Shipbuilders at one time inscribed the name and statistics of a ship on such a nail, implanting it as described.

Unfortunately, "the divers had difficulty digging up the forward end of the keel from under four to five feet of muck and rubble. When they did, they found the stem had rotted at the point where it joined the keel, where the nail would have been imbedded."

Extensive research through musty files in the British patent offices revealed the rotted windlass to be of a type patented in 1829 and manufactured for 15 years. Even Lloyds of London had contributed by searching its old shipping registers.

But, to date, the battered wreck's secret remains as much a mystery as the summer of 1958 when Dr. Cottrell's expedition found her in Sydney Inlet.

Similar discoveries have intrigued historians and the curious over the years. In December of 1962, army and navy divers found a large, barnacle-encrusted anchor off Esquimalt Lagoon, near Victoria, during a routine diving exercise.

"It was the biggest thrill any of us has had," said Lt.-Cmdr. C.P. Ilsley, stating that the anchor's wooden stock dated it as being between 150 and 175 years old. Winched from 30 feet of water, the rusted anchor and 90 feet of chain aroused hopes of finding a wreck nearby.

Subsequent research indicated the anchor—unique to Pacific Northwest experts as its stock was rounded, rather than squared—to be of more recent vintage, possibly from one of four sailing ships driven ashore during a vicious sou'easter, April 14, 1883. The *Connaught, Tiber, Gettysburg* and *Southern Chief* had been badly mauled, the *Cannaught* having to be declared a total loss.

Months after this discovery, Campbell River skindivers located a wreck off Shelter Point, recovering a 10-foot anchor and chain. Newspaper reports of the find brought forward a Victorian who identified the hulk as that of a square-rigger beached off Shelter Point after striking a reef during the First World War. He could not recall her name, said Richard Larson, but he believed she had been transporting settlers and supplies to Alaska.

Unfortunately, once the crew and passengers had struggled safely ashore with most of their possessions intact, they had entrusted them to the care of a local man. Among the salvaged cargo had been a keg of rum, and when survivors had returned days later, they found their goods and watchman gone—and the keg empty.

Other victims of earlyday storm and reef intrigue adventurous skindivers from time to time. Some, such as the 2,200-ton *Pass of Melfort,* which went down with all hands off Amphitrite Point at the entrance to Ucluelet Harbor, Christmas night, 1905, can be identified through old records and on-the-spot investigation.

But the sea seldom allows man more than a peak into her dark depths and so many of her mysteries must remain forever unsolved.

Chapter 2

Alpha's *Owners Answered Call of Easy Riches*

Shadows draw a murky veil over the reefs forming the rocky perch of Yellow Rock, where the little steamer *Alpha* died 70 years ago. Here, in the depths at the southern tip of Denman Island, the ill-fated ship's skeleton is to be found yet, home of ling cod and prowling octopus. Waving streamers of kelp grow from her scattered bones, enacting a dance of death, three-quarters of a century after she tore out her bottom in a maelstrom of wind and wave, carrying nine men down with her.

Alpha had known better days before she joined the Klondike treasure fleet. Built on the Clyde for Cunard Steamships in 1863, the 700-tonner ran the Atlantic gauntlet between Nova Scotia and the West Indies, continuing on the same route as mail steamer when purchased by Pickford and Black of Halifax.

In 1898 her owners answered the siren call of easy riches from the stormy North Pacific, where bottoms of every size and condition were in desperate demand to carry adventurers to the Klondike gold fields.

The Victoria *Daily Colonist* of July 6, 1898, reported her arrival after a three-month voyage via the Straights of Magellan: "A big white steamer with tall, graceful spars and neat appearance, with flush deck and comparatively little housework, is the *Alpha,* a steamer which yesterday arrived from Halifax..."

Tragedy had befallen the ship in May, when anchored off Punta Delgada on the Argentinian coast. Four young seamen had rowed ashore to pick up a pilot. They were pulling back to the steamer when capsized by a large sea, as their shipmates watched in horror. "It was 10 o'clock in the morning and the weather was rainy and squally. A five-knot current was running and with these the men stood no show for life."

11

Captain Hall had instantly ordered a boat launched, but the rescue party "accomplished nothing…not even the boat could be recovered, although three hours of hard work was spent. The accident entirely marred the pleasure of the voyage," said the *Colonist*.

Sighed Mrs. Hall, the master's wife, "It would otherwise have been pleasant, but this affair seemed to make the voyage a gloomy one."

Alpha was to know misfortune more than once during her brief West Coast career. Placed on the Victoria-Alaska run, she completed her first voyage that September, returning with more than 100 passengers and a fortune in gold. Among her prominent passengers were J. Schmelzel, owner of 45 Eldorado claim, who carried $10,000; Paul Kimball, with $25,000; and Kelly, the "Duke of Moosehide," with an unrecorded treasure.

Alpha made several successful voyages in this service, her decks knowing the heavy tread of successful miner, heartbroken failure and the hopeful cheechako. Among her passengers in June of 1899 was Nova Scotian Jacob Boutlier, one of three survivors of a party of nine which had headed for the gold fields over the Edmonton Trail. Months later, Boutlier, laborer J.L. Dunbrack, and Seaman Frank Johnson had staggered from the wilderness at Dease Lake, suffering from exhaustion, exposure and scurvy.

Earlier, the trio had elected to forge ahead, their companions agreeing to "follow leisurely the trail left by their guide party, and did so until a late January snowstorm obliterated the path-marks and left them to perish in the wilds."

When search parties valiantly battled winter blizzards without sign of the missing adventurers, a saddened and destitute Boutlier proceeded to Wrangell, where he was given free passage to Victoria on the *Alpha* by Captain J.D. Warren. Dunbrack remained in the Glenora hospital, "so low with fever and scurvy that it is doubtful if he will emerge alive."

A second free guest of Captain Warren was A.S. Fletcher of Boston, whose partner had succumbed of scurvy on the Glenora trail.

Another eventful passage occurred in July, when a Halifax passenger named Hernon, maddened by delirium tremens, had to be handcuffed and locked in a cabin. Four days out, he asked his guard for a plate of soup, using the watchman's brief absence to cut his throat with a straight razor. Fortunately, *Alpha* listed a doctor among her passengers on this voyage, and hapless Hernon's life was saved.

Despite her 35 years, Ss. *Alpha* was popular, as evidenced by the fact passengers twice signed petitions expressing "our thanks for the considerate treatment accorded us by her worthy commander, Captain J.D. Warren and his officers.

"We heartily commend this boat and its officers and crew to any and all parties who may take this trip between these two ports, deeming her a stout, speedy ship, kindly manned and officered, and sailed with great care."

In October, 1899, Canadian and American seamen speculated "as to how successful the steamer *Alpha* will be on the voyage to St. Michael." Captain Warren and mate Otto Buckholtz apparently had gambled they could complete a final trip that season, despite the assurances of collegues that Cape Nome would be iced in. Five weeks later *Alpha* steamed triumphantly into Victoria after a "rough voyage," although she had, to everyone's astonishment, encountered no ice.

Amid nasty rumors to the effect Captain Warren had landed Canadian-made goods at Nome without informing Alaskan customs, *Alpha's* owners proceeded to have her cabin space enlarged.

With December, sporting types already were wagering as to which steamer would capture the honor of being first into Nome with the spring thaw. Former first mate Otto Buckholtz, now master of the *Alpha,* vowed to win the laurels, planning to penetrate the 650-mile icefield through experience gained aboard the Dundee whalers off Greenland, and "two years' " study in a big observatory in Berlin."

Although he would not "disclose his plans in their entirety" to a Victoria reporter, Captain Buckholtz did say he enjoyed complete confidence in *Alpha's* inch-thick iron hull, maintaining a steel bottom "would smash like glass in the cold."

Alpha's owners obviously shared Buckholtz's enthusiasm, having the steamer refitted that month.

Early that spring, Alpha steamed northward. But the headlines the old liner made were not in connection with the race to Nome. For this time she had unquestionably landed Canadian merchandise in violation of United States customs. When Captain Buckholtz steamed back to Victoria, he learned his command had been formally charged with smuggling. *Alpha's* owners defended her actions strenuously in Seattle court, but in vain. The verdict was guilty; if ever *Alpha* entered an American port, she would be seized and sold.

It meant the finish of *Alpha's* busy Alaskan career. Limited to service between Canadian ports, she was placed on the northern B.C. route. When canning season ended, her owners unsuccessfully sought other charters, then tried selling her. But no one wanted poor *Alpha;* she had become a white elephant.

Worse, she had become a floating nightmare. Only months before, she had been eulogized by contented passengers. Now even her own officers and crew cursed her rusting plates and cranky steering. The many years and Arctic ice had taken their toll of the dowager.

Consequently, her owners decided to sell her in the Orient, the last service of many a dying ship.

Early in December of 1900, *Alpha* limped from Victoria's outer wharf with 500 tons of salted salmon for Yokohama. Days later, she was back at her dock, "with three of her crew working the hand pumps continuously to keep water down in her flooded engine and fire rooms; her feed-pipe is disabled, and there are some other minor repairs necessary."

The *Colonist* learned little from Captain F.H. Yorke or owner Samuel Barber beyond the fact she had suddenly begun flooding 200 miles at sea, and had had to race back to port, only her hand pumps keeping her afloat as her steam pumps had been disabled. Upon docking, her engineers had been standing at their stations in 18 inches of water.

The following day, her machinery was repaired, although marine surveyors still had not found the leak.

December 12, the newspaper reported, "The troubles of the steamer *Alpha* grow apace. Likewise the stories concerning them. The engineers have left, and now the crew are endeavoring to have the vessel held or to be given a discharge from her. As they have been paid in advance, the owners naturally object to their going.

"On Monday a number of the crew, accompanied by a lawyer, went to Collector A.R. Milne and asked him to refuse to grant a clearance until the vessel was surveyed. This, he told them, he could not do. If they wanted to take action against the steamer in this connection, the only course was for them to leave her, and when tried for desertion, as they could be on such action, endeavor to prove any alleged unseaworthiness."

The seamen protested to Shipping Master H.G. Lewis, also, despite surveyors' reports that *Alpha* was structurally sound.

"According to a local mariner, who has looked over the vessel, the water seen in her fire room and engine room on her arrival, which kept the pumps busy for some time, did not come into the vessel from any leakage through the plates of the vessel, but through a valve of one of the pipes in the mechanism of the engine room of the craft. The water came in through this connection, and now that the cause of the leakage has been found and repaired, there is no water coming into this vessel."

Despite this assurance, *Alpha's* crew protested bitterly, as Captain Yorke announced she would sail immediately. Came the hour of departure, Chief Engineer W. Gordon and Second Engineer Shires — and half of the crew — were not to be found.

Owner Barber then conferred with senior partner Genelle, of Vancouver, the two deciding to press charges against the deserting crew, and alleging that *Alpha's* sea cock had been deliberately opened.

Engineer Gordon immediately visited the *Colonist* to "deny the assertion," where he was arrested. When neither his junior, Shires, nor the seamen were picked up, Captain Yorke managed to scrap

14

together replacements in Vancouver and Puget Sound ports, local mariners apparently being uninterested.

In court, Gordon "made a disconnected statement from the box, in which he said the ship was not seaworthy; the firemen were incompetent; there was no load water line or Plimsol mark on the steamer, and that she was loaded too deep. She took water, he said, when she rolled and that the captain himself had admitted this at Steveston.

"The fault, he thought, lay in one of the sea connections, which was too low. This, he said, was a matter for the boiler and not the hull inspector."

In sentencing him to 10 days' imprisonment, the magistrate said he had not proved his charges and was therefore guilty of desertion.

At 5:00 the next morning, Ss *Alpha* finally left her pier with 700 tons of salmon and no pilot. Two days later, electrifying word of her foundering swept the city. "Nine men lost!" cried *Colonist* headlines, reporting the accursed steamer had been lost in Baynes Sound and that Captain Yorke and Samuel Barber were among the drowned.

Initial reports indicated Captain Yorke, caught in a vicious gale which pounded the entire Northwest, had piled up his steamer at the base of Yellow Island lighthouse while enroute to Union Bay for coal. Among the missing were the owner's brother, J.H. Barber, purser, and the replacement engineers.

Full details were learned two weeks later, when first mate W.B. Wilkinson reached Victoria. Ironically he reported, had not overheated bearings caused a two-and-a-half-hour delay off Pender Island, *Alpha* would have navigated Baynes Sound in daylight, thereby, in all probability, escaping disaster.

The storm had struck at 4 p.m., December 15, Captain Yorke saying he would make for Yellow Island, get his bearings from the lighthouse, then put about for shelter. Two hours later, Wilkinson hurried to the bridge, to ask, "Are you not going to shove her around?"

Yorke replied he would proceed as planned, and steamed on into the raging darkness. Time and again, Wilkinson pleaded with his superior to put about, Yorke refusing until at last the lighthouse's pencil-like beacon was sighted, when he seemed to lose his nerve, "porting and starboarding his helm, first one and then the other."

Desperately, the chief officer demanded they turn back. Without answering, Yorke "walked to the far side of the bridge, and shouted an order to the helmsman to 'Hard astarboard!' These were the last words the captain was heard to utter by the first officer, other than a request to get his chronometer, when the steamer struck. The helmsman had replied, when the order was given, that the helm was already hard astarboard, and Mr. Wilkinson had looked and found this to be true."

Moments later, *Alpha* bounded into the reef, shuddered heavily, and toppled Wilkinson. Regaining his feet, he stared into the blackness, spotting a seaman named Anderson as he dropped over the side with the heaving line tied about his waist. "There was no talk on Anderson's part or marked sentiment. He had known his duty, and picking up the rope, went over into the darkness, to what, he did not know."

Miraculously, the courageous sailor landed on the rocks without serious injury. Running to the foot of the cliffs, he hauled in a three-inch hawser and secured it about a tall rock. His daring act had taken but minutes, although it had seemed an eternity to those aboard the grinding steamer, who were sure he had perished in the breakers.

"Anderson had scarcely got ashore when the steamer, which was resting on the rock as on a pivot, swerved around broadside to the gale, and acted like a breakwater to the high seas, which rolled over her from side to side until her rails were below water. The wind by then had reached hurricane force, and the great green seas were breaking right over the swinging vessel."

Somehow two more seamen managed to make shore with auxiliary lines which were stretched alongside the hawser. During the next two-and-a-half hours, 28 men crawled to safety. Throughout the ordeal, Wilkinson had urged Captain Yorke, the Barbers, and six others to make the attempt. Four times Yorke tried crossing the snaking lines unsuccessfully; the Barbers each tried three times.

As the ship rolled drunkenly, the lifelines would whip taut, then instantly slacken when towering waves swept the disintegrating hulk back, toward the rocks. Making conditions even worse for those still aboard, because of the darkness they could not be sure their comrades had reached shore.

Finally, Wilkinson knew he could delay no longer. With a last entreaty to those clinging, panic-stricken, to *Alpha's* rigging, he "swung down into the sea and up in the air, but managed to make his way over the lines without more injury than a few bruises."

Then began a torturous, two-hour death watch, the shivering, battered survivors watching from the rocks as old *Alpha* was steadily hammered beneath the waves. "For two hours afterwards the forms could be seen in the rigging, and their heart-rending cries and shrieks could be heard as the wind carried the sound right to them.

"It was at 1:07 that the nine men were swept to death. They could be seen huddled in the rigging after the seas swept over them, until then, with one great shriek, they were dashed with the broken mast into the roaring waters."

The end had come for ancient Ss. *Alpha.*

On January 3, 1901, a coroner's inquest at Cumberland found Captain Yorke negligent in having attempted to make an unfamiliar port in the storm without a pilot, also criticizing the fact that the steamer's chart had been 40 years old.

Chapter 3

Ss Cleveland *Led a Charmed Life*

She was old, tender and cranky, and marine underwriters shuddered at the very thought of her. Yet Ss. *Cleveland* was one of the very few ships to come to grief in Vancouver Island's dreaded Graveyard of the Pacific — and live.

Three-quarters of a century later, *Cleveland*, like so many of her sisters, is long gone and forgotten; few remembering the day she made history...and men died.

Launched as the *Sirius* in 1865, the 1,160-ton brigantine-rigged steamer *Cleveland* had sailed most of the seven seas under various names and flags during her 32 years. By the time she joined the Northwest fleet she was not, like the fabled grey mare, "what she used to be." Only the starved demand for bottoms — any and all — during the Klondike rush kept her employed. Although when she crashed onto Trial Island, off Victoria, while engaged in the Nanaimo coal trade, even her stubborn owners thought it time to retire her.

Her master had been content to leave her high and dry rather than pay salvage costs when a freak change of wind swung her free with little damage for yet another lease on life.

First word that something was wrong came on December 14, 1897, when the *City of Puebla* docked in Victoria without word of the overdue freighter. A week behind schedule on her run from San Francisco, she had caused concern here and in Seattle. As each day passed, only her agent, Captain E.E. Caine, remained confident that the venerable lady had survived a series of wild gales which had swept the Northwest.

Two days later, headlines told the grim story: She was a total wreck in Barkley Sound, most of her crew missing and presumed lost. Word of the disaster had reached Victoria through the efforts of Purser J.W. Whitbeck "after an experience such as few men endure and live."

The life-and-death battle had begun at 10:30 p.m., December 6, when the *Cleveland* was beating her way up the Oregon coast, off Columbia River, in a raging sou'easter. For hours, Capt. Charles F. Hall had kept his ancient command on course despite the opposing wind. But at 10:30 the worst occurred — a broken propeller shaft. Instantly, *Cleveland* wallowed helplessly, and Captain Hall got sail on her in hopes of working the ship near enough to Cape Flattery to hail a cruising tug.

None was sighted, but early the next morning she spoke the schooner *Marion*, whose master promised to report her plight to the first steamer he met.

"The wind continued to blow," recalled Purser Whitbeck, "then changed suddenly — the ship drifting toward Cape Flattery, which light was sighted on Wednesday morning at 2 o'clock." For six hours *Cleveland's* anxious crew fired one rocket after another. She received no reply from the lighthouse, no help came.

Cleveland continued drifting northward. Off Cape Beale, on Vancouver Island's west coast, her company once again signalled distress. Although the gale continued as strongly as ever, the weather was clear. But, strangely, as at Flattery, Cape Beale light did not acknowledge their signals; they remained alone.

"By this time," Whitbeck continued in the third person, "the ship was rapidly nearing the breakers of Starlight Reef. The case began to look desperate, and the boats having been thoroughly provisioned and equipped (not thoroughly enough, as they were to learn to their sorrow), were lowered and manned; First Officer S. B. Durfee, Second Officer Henderson and Third Officer (Harry) Melvin each in charge of one.

"These were dropped astern, the fourth boat being kept alongside, awaiting Captain Hall, who remained on the bridge until the ship was within 150 yards of the reef, when he decided that there was no hope of saving his vessel and took to the boat, having previously given orders to the other boats to cast off their lines, keep close together, and follow him.

"All then stood by until the ship drifted among the breakers and out of sight. They then pulled to the eastward, only to encounter a strong current setting in to the northwest, which took them to the westward of Shelter Island. The captain's boat waited for the others to come up, and then signalled for them to follow through Alpha Passage. The skipper and his companions succeeded in making the somewhat hazardous passage — utilizing three cans of oil to keep the seas from breaking in the boat astern and no doubt saving it from destruction — and in landing safely, but none of the other boats have,

18

since the signals were exchanged, been seen or heard of."

The purser's straightforward account does little justice to the horrors he and comrades had experienced in rowing ashore. Deep in the rock-studded waters of Barkley Sound, in a tiny rowboat during one of the worst gales in pioneer memory, their escape from drowning had been nothing less than miraculous.

After resting, the shipwrecked mariners scoured adjacent beaches for signs of their missing companions. Nothing. Worried, although not alarmed, they began hiking for help, finally reaching the Ucluelet home of John Margotitch, where they waited until the savage gale had at last subsided. Then, with Margotitch, they searched Shelter Island. This time, to their dismay, they found signs of their shipmates. Littering a beach were most of the provisions which had been so carefully stored in the lifeboats. Captain Hall and seven companions expressed the faint hope that the others had landed safely, although fearing the worst.

They were back at Ucluelet when Rev. Melvin Swartout brought word that *Cleveland* was ashore and intact. Hastily, six of the survivors returned to their late command, leaving Chief Engineer Husar and passenger Lathbury recuperating from exposure at the settlement. The sailors boarded without difficulty, to be greeted by a sight that was almost beyond belief.

Cleveland "was standing in tolerably fair condition...her holds filled with water (and) the craft looked like a forsaken waif of the sea."

But it was not the damage of the storm which fascinated the seamen. During their 48-hour absence, Indians had boarded the derelict and embarked on an orgy of looting. "The vessel had in fact been ransacked from stem to stern, and in the short time at their disposal the predatory Siwashes had removed everything portable, even to the ship's furniture and fixtures, all instruments and navigation books, together with the personal effects of officers, passengers and crew.

"Next they had given attention to the cargo, at least 100 tons of which is roughly estimated to have been carried away. More would no doubt have gone had not the Indians at this juncture struck the whiskey to which they proceeded to give undivided attention. The cased goods were immediately appropriated and then the store of bulk liquor was tapped, and such of the general cargo as could not be removed scattered about the deck."

Worse, in hopes of destroying evidence of their depredations, the drunken pirates had attempted firing the ship. Besides trying to take inventory of the damages, Captain Hall and exhausted company were twice engaged in extinguishing the flames.

It was then Hall resolved to send Purser Whitbeck for aid. Hiring two Indians and a canoe at Cape Beale, Whitbeck began his 200-mile race for help. It nearly ended in disaster when his guides turned out to have been among the buccaneers who had looted the *Cleveland*. Whitbeck drew this conclusion when the braves, still feeling the effects of the firewater, upset the canoe, throwing all into the frigid sea.

For two hours the shivering purser and his still drunken guides had wrestled with the craft, finally swimming ashore with it in tow. When the boat was ready, Whitbeck found his companions still incapacitated and returned to the village. The next morning he and two seamen, accompanied by John Margotitch and his son, rowed to Alberni, 50 miles distant.

Once again Whitbeck met with disappointment. He had intended telegraphing word of the disaster to Victoria, but found the line out of service due to an incompetent operator at Parksville having left his key open.

"In view of this he determined to push on himself to Victoria...and at three the purser started on his ride through the forest stopping only for change of horses until Nanaimo was reached." Twelve hours later!

At the coal city Whitbeck boarded the train. At Chemainus, his "good fairy," as the *Colonist* described it, once again came to his aid, and readers marvelled at the extraordinary coincidence through which Whitbeck finally sent aid to his shipmates.

During the stop at Chemainus, the harried purser had seen, from his coach window, a ship anchored in the harbor. Informed she was the lighthouse tender *Quadra*, Whitbeck fervently moaned, "If only I could see her captain or agent for a moment!"

To which a fellow passenger replied, "That won't be difficult, for I'm going to Victoria by this train, too."

The passenger then introduced himself as Captain James Gaudin, agent of marine. The overjoyed purser breathlessly told him of the *Cleveland's* plight and Gaudin instructed the station master to inform *Quadra's* commander, Captain John T. Walbran, to await further orders.

At Duncan, Gaudin wired Walbran to "fly" to Victoria where he would meet him, and, that night, DGS *Quadra* steamed to the rescue. Aboard were Purser Whitbeck, Captain Gaudin, U.S. Vice-Consul Sidney W. Smith, Captain R. Collister, provincial inspector of hulls; Captain John Irving, MPP; Superintendent Fred Hussey of the provincial police, and a diver. The steamer *Willapa* cleared harbor at the same time with instructions to save what she could of *Cleveland's* cargo.

Upon arrival, *Quadra's* party found the Alberni Indian agent and two constables on the scene to prevent further acts of piracy by the natives. A private steam launch had already begun the search for *Cleveland's* overdue crewmen, as the tugs *Lorne* and *Wanderer* reached the wreck.

"The wrecked *Cleveland* is today a dismal object of endless speculation to marine men who look upon her," wrote a marvelling reporter, and "a wonder to them in more ways than one. In the first place because of her remarkable drift to a spot apparently in the centre of the archipelago, and again because of the marked diversity of opinion as to the feasibility of again putting her afloat.

"She is to the landman's eye a picture of dilapidation, and worst of all, everything at present seems to indicate that the 22 missing members of her company will not be seen again in this life."

Quadra immediately commenced a thorough sweep of the immediate bays and inlets. But there was not a sign of *Cleveland's* missing boats, and Captain Walbran surmised they had been blown northward to Clayoquot Sound. Indian agent Guillod and the constables in the meantime rounded up all looting suspects and recovered most of the ship's property and cargo.

Constable Cox had found Captain Hall and companions in a sad state, as they had spent two days and nights aboard without food or even a blanket. What the Indians had not carried away they had maliciously destroyed with knife and axe. Only upon Cox's arrival did Captain Hall "get my first real sleep in nine days.

"Although I only snatched a half-hour from duty, it seemed that I had been in dreamland for weeks, so refreshed was I."

While waiting for the weather to clear to continue the search, Captain Walbran turned his attention to arresting Indians suspected of stripping the ship. More days passed without sign of the overdue seamen and their grieving comrades aboard *Cleveland* now held little hope of their being found alive.

Then, on December 20 — a miracle! Thirteen of the lost crew had been found!

Father A.J. Brabant of Hesquiat had sent word that Third Mate Melvin's boat had reached his mission safely. First Officer Durfee's boat was found at Rafael Point, 15 miles away, the following day by Indians. Only George Carillo, steward, had not survived their nightmare. Of Second Officer Henderson's crew, eight in all, there was not a trace.

"There is rejoicing, tempered with sadness, on board the *Quadra*," Purser Whitbeck wired Victoria. "Rejoicing, because 13 of our ship's family have been given back by the seas. Sadness, because eight of those who, with us, sailed from San Francisco two weeks ago, are lost beyond further hope.

"Leaving the scene of the wreck at noon on Friday, the *Quadra*, later in the same day, found the third officer's boat at Hesquoit (sic) with Harry Melvin and his companions well cared for and fast recovering their strength at the home of the good priest, Father Brabant... This morning, after a terrible battle with the wind and sea, the agonies of which no pen can picture…we received them on board the *Quadra* and continued the search for the others of the first boat.

"The Indians had heard that there was a fire on the beach and a broken boat at Rafael Point, 15 miles or so away, and thither the cutter went at once, although the sea was still dangerously high and a bad surf running. The Indians' report proved, happily, a true one, for on the morning of Wednesday, the 15th, boat number two, in charge of First Officer Durfee, had come ashore, and Durfee and his companions dragged themselves up on the rocks where they lay exhausted.

"Poor George Carillo, the second steward, died of exposure in a dementia induced by intense strain, suffering, cold and hunger. His body was sorrowfully dipped into the seas on Wednesday, the 15th. Some of the rescued men in boat number two are still suffering severely from their long exposure, but the officers of the *Quadra* have extended such unreserved hospitality that under the circumstances they could be no more comfortable if they were at home."

Captain Walbran sped the suffering survivors to Alberni for medical attention as other ships continued the hopeless hunt for Second Officer Henderson and company.

The three lifeboats had become separated with that of Captain Hall almost immediately upon leaving the *Cleveland*. In the "riots of the elements," they had misinterpreted his frenzied signals to follow him through Alpha Passage. Upon realizing their error, it had been too late.

"In the moment of excitement and great danger the oil cans were forgotten, and the breakers unchecked threatened momentarily to demolish all three boats. Try as they would the shipwrecked seamen could not keep toward shore; steadily the persistent wind drove them to sea, and to northward until they were forced to a realization of their fate — to be carried, helpless to resist, wherever the storm king willed."

Without compass or chart, most of their precious food supply swept away, the mates could not estimate their positions. Then they too were separated. Durfee's boat was leaking so badly two men had to bail around the clock to keep her afloat. In shifts, the terrified mariners fought the rising water for four and a-half days. Then their tiny store of sea biscuit and water was gone and starvation became the new enemy.

Ailing steward Carillo, ill before leaving the ship, deteriorated rapidly. Propped against a coil of rope in the stern, ice cold water to his chest, he had early lapsed into a delirium, "talking of home and friends, while his comrades labored with dull hopelessness toward they knew not where."

The driving gale pressed them ever northward.

Durfee's boat had been blown within sight of Ucluelet. Desperately, the suffering crew raised oars against the storm but it was hopeless. Waving jackets frantically and shouting until hoarse, they saw the little town vanish astern. No one had seen them, they were still alone.

Durfee then decided they must land, "even if it were at the price of death in the surf," for their boat was sinking under them. Providence finally smiled on the castaways, bringing them ashore at Rafael Point, somehow surviving the immense breakers. Their boat smashed, "like a discarded plaything, the sailors lay like dead men on the rocky beach.

"Two of the men had broken limbs which could not be set; fire was unobtainable; nor any food save the mussels, which they dragged themselves up the rocks and hungrily devoured. Finally Indians came, built a fire, dried their clothes and gave them food — caring for them with solicitude in strong contrast with the conduct of their Barkley Sound neighbors." When DGS *Quadra* picked them up, Durfee could only murmur: "God bless the *Quadra*." Later asked by Captain Walbran of his adventures, he replied, "I am too glad to speak."

Third Officer Melvin's party had fared considerably better, being adrift only three days when a benevolent fate landed them at Hesquiat. Gracious Father Brabant, combining "a limited knowledge of medicine and simple surgery with his spiritual ministrations," soon had the seamen recuperating.

When both parties boarded *Quadra*, few showed little sign of their ordeal. Four sailors needed immediate hospitalization, suffering from exposure, exhaustion, hunger and blood poisoning. Of the rest, several were unable to walk, although all were expected to recover satisfactorily.

On December 22, *Quadra* brought the first mate's party to Victoria, six of whom were admitted to the marine hospital. Also aboard the cutter were six Indian prisoners, tried and convicted by Walbran, who had power of magistrate, of looting tragic *Cleveland*.

From his hospital bed Mate Durfee told how he and company had survived on eight cans of food, mouldy biscuit and little water. When they had at last staggered ashore, they found a cave and took shelter in its damp confines until sighted by passing Indians and rescued by the *Quadra*. It had been "the most terrible experience" of his life.

Salvaged, Ss. *Cleveland* returned to service for several further unhappy years, experiencing grounding and near-wreck. Once, out of coal, her fires had been fed by furniture and fittings until the ill-starred craft struggled into port.

Cleveland's missing seamen were never found alive. It is ironic that her men had abandoned ship as they would have been safe had they remained aboard. But in that hell of wind and wave, Captain Hall had been sure she would be smashed to pieces in the breakers.

Another melancholy feature of the tragedy was the fact her officers had had no idea of their positions. With any knowledge of the region they would have been able to make safe landings earlier with less suffering. But the very fact their cockleshell boats had survived in the notorious Pacific Graveyard is a miracle which caused mariners to shake their heads in solemn wonder.

As anyone familiar with this treacherous expanse of Vancouver Island's west coast can only do today.

Chapter 4

Romance Aboard Wrecked Consort

Shipwreck on the jagged Pacific coast could involve more than hardship and death, in the romantic age of sail. Heartbreak of a very different nature attended such tragedies more than once; an intriguing example is the wreck of the brig *Consort*, in 1860.

"The town was thrown into a state of unwonted excitement at 2 o'clock yesterday afternoon, by the announcement that HM Gunboat *Forward* had been seen off Trial Island, heading for this port," reported the *Colonist*, on January 16, 1861.

"About 4 o'clock she was seen slowly entering the harbor under steam. The glad news spread rapidly, and the Hudson's Bay Company's wharf was soon lined with spectators, who expressed in strong terms the intense satisfaction they felt at seeing the gallant little vessel and her crew again in our harbor. Several boats filled with friends were soon on their way towards her, and boarded her when she cast anchor, in order that they might be among the first to welcome their friends home again."

The reason for Victoria's "intense satisfaction" upon the gunboat's return was the fact she and her brave company, under command of Lieutenant Charles R. Robson, had been given up as lost. Last sign of HMS *Forward* had been when she cleared port, weeks before, in search of the distressed bridgantine *Florencia*. Then — nothing.

Weeks had passed without word of the overdue gunboat; weeks during which the coast was lashed again and again by winter gales. But days after *Forward* had sailed upon her errand of mercy, in fact, one extraordinarily savage storm had rampaged for three days and nights, bludgeoning several sailing craft beneath the waves. As more time went by, local mariners "got down the charts and compasses and began to calculate where the *Forward* ought to be at such and such a date if she had not gone to the bottom."

This exercise led only to increased apprehension, navigators glumly agreeing that HMS *Forward* had had time to circumnavigate Vancouver Island. By all accounts, she should have returned — if she remained afloat. When surveying ships *Plumper* and *Hecate* completed a vain sweep of the Island's west coast, few remained optimistic.

Finally, on the happy afternoon of January 15, word had swept the city that the gunboat was off Trial Island. Hence the crowds which had lined the HBC wharf, and the flotilla of rowboats that eagerly surrounded the long lost warship.

After the excitement abated somewhat, Lieutenant Robson gave a brief account of the eventful cruise. Upon arrival at Nootka, he had met the disabled *Florencia* as planned. He also found an urgent letter. Addressed to "friends of humanity," the scribbled note was signed by a Captain McLellan, who reported his ship, the American brig *Consort*, bound from Honolulu to Puget Sound, had wrecked at the entrance to Quatsino Sound. Sixteen persons, including three women and two children, had made it to shore, wrote McLellan, where they were "subsisting on clams and fish and such edible articles as came ashore from the wreck." Suffering from hunger and exposure, the shipwrecked crew required immediate aid.

As the Indian messenger's canoe had been delayed by continuing storms, the letter was 12 days old when handed aboard the *Forward* at Nootka. Worse, the stranded company had been on the inhospitable beach since November 15.

Immediately clearing for Cape Scott, HMS *Forward* steamed into San Josef Bay and picked up the stricken 16, returning to Nootka to take the ailing *Florencia* in tow for Victoria. But the little convoy was not long at sea when mauled by yet another gale.

Then, to make matters worse, *Forward's* frail boiler broke down. Throwing on canvas, Lieutenant Robson had no choice but to abandon the brig's towline and claw his own way to safety. In the dark maelstrom, *Florencia's* crew misinterpreted the gunboat's signal to put about for Friendly Cove. Instead, thinking Robson's order was to take in their mainsail, the merchantmen proceeded to obey, and, minutes later, were alone in the gale.

Sadly, it meant the end of doughty *Florencia*, the brig crashing ashore on the small island near Ucluelet which today bears her name. But that is another story, and to return to courageous *Forward* and her company of castaways:

Upon reaching Friendly Cove, the recalcitrant boiler was repaired, although engineers were unable to restore full steam pressure, with the result that, when *Forward* again limped to sea, it was under canvas.

For three days, Robson attempted to beat southward against the storm, but without success, finally deciding to head northward around the Island, and down the Inside Passage to Victoria.

Restoring at Fort Rupert (150 pounds of potatoes and a single sack of flour) *Forward* proceeded under steam and sail to Nanaimo, where crew and castaways, by this time on rations, probably enjoyed hearty meals. Even during the last leg of her epic voyage, *Forward* encountered stiff head winds, which gave her balky engines further grief.

However, the good gunboat at last sailed into Victoria's Inner Harbor, scarred but safe, to discharge her grateful passengers, Captain McLellan, Chief Officer John Lockman, his wife and child, a male passenger, and 11 crewmen. All deeply appreciated Lieutenant Robson's care, thanking him "in terms of the warmest gratitude, for his gallant and humane conduct, from first to last."

As all but two passengers were left destitute, wearing only the ill-fitting clothes members of *Forward's* crew had been able to spare them, Victorians subscribed to a fund, collecting $200 "in a few minutes." MP William J. McDonald opened his home to Mate Lockman and his family, the others being established in a hotel. Because several of the crew "suffered from a want of food" the first night, police officers generously treated them to dinner in the barracks.

Captain McLellan then told of the harrowing events leading up to the loss of his ship. Clearing Honolulu October 6, they had proceeded without incident to within 800 miles of the Washington coast, when dismasted in a stiff gale. Rigging jury masts, *Consort* limped onward. Eleven cruel days later, the old brig sighted Cape Flattery light, when the sadistic wind whipped around, to buffet her from the southeast, and drive her back to sea.

When her lookout spotted the San Francisco bark *Glimpse*, beating towards the mouth of Juan de Fuca Strait, Captain McLellan ordered distress signals displayed. For hours the bark advanced steadily, those aboard the disabled brig congratulating each other upon their early rescue. But it was not to be. Within a mile of them, the *Glimpse* crossed their bow, then continued on to Cape Flattery. She had not seen them.

"The brig was then driven to and fro by the wind and waves, and on the 15th of November was driven ashore near the northern end of the Island. A raft was made and a hawser sent ashore, by means of which they all reached dry land safely. They stopped at the point where they were wrecked until the 29th of November, when, by the advice of some Indians, they repaired to a native settlement...where, on the 18th of December, the gunboat arrived and took them on board.

"Mrs. Lockman, the only female passenger on board the *Consort*, bore up bravely during the whole of the trying scenes through which she was compelled to pass, and received great praise for the fortitude she displayed on all occasions."

For five bitter weeks, the castaways had survived in a crude shelter of pine boughs, through which winter wind and rain "found easy passage," until at last rescued.

That, according to the somewhat sketchy newspaper columns of that date, is the story of the wreck of the good ship *Consort*; one shipwreck of B.C.'s evil coast which ended happily.

It was not until 45 years later that pioneer journalist David W. Higgins recalled the story within a story concerning the brig *Consort*. Although his version differs substantially from that told above, and Mr. Higgins changed the names to avoid embarrassment, modern researchers generally enjoy the greatest confidence in his accuracy. For, although this master scribe made the odd error in dates and the like, his recollections of early-day B.C. are unexcelled. Whenever a story broke, Mr. Higgins was on hand, pen at the ready. His amazing experiences, told in two books and many newspaper features, provide one of the best insights into the people and events which founded the colony that today forms Canada's westernmost province.

This is the story Mr. Higgins recalled upon retirement, 70 years ago:

Among the *Consort's* passengers on that fateful last voyage were two men, three ladies, and two children. The gentlemen were Honolulu sugar merchants, one lady passenger and the children the family of Captain McLellan (or Captain "Blanchard," as Mr. Higgins named him). The two remaining ladies were — "well, no one on board knew who they were, exactly."

Not that the brig's crew hadn't invested considerable speculation, as both ladies were young and very attractive — even if one was the other's mother. A widow, she appeared to be about 32 years of age, the daughter about 20.

As few seemed to have marvelled at this slight difference in ages, readers can only conclude that they married young, a century ago!

When the mate, a handsome young dandy whom Mr. Higgins dubbed "John Walters," did express curiousity as to the apparent discrepancy in years, by joking that "Mrs. Forbes" looked much too young to have a daughter of 20, that amazing lady replied with surprising candor that appearances were deceiving — she was 39.

Perhaps this refreshing honesty (not to mention her looks) provided the spark of love. Whatever, Mate Walters fell head over heels for his fair passenger — within two days' of sailing. It should, perhaps, be stressed here, for the benefit of those who may not have been paying attention, that the object of impulsive Walters' ardor was not the lovely Miss Forbes, but her mother!

A week out, Walters proposed and Mrs. Forbes, 14 years his senior, accepted.

One tropical evening, Mrs. McLellan (or Mrs. Blanchard, to quote Mr. Higgins) was resting on deck on her rattan settee. Nearby, oblivious to her presence, the young lovers were whispering sweet nothings. As the captain's better half listened eagerly, Walters made the engagement official by slipping his seal ring upon his intended's finger with a vow to replace it with a solitaire diamond upon landing.

"The next morning," the journalist continued, "it was evident that a coolness had sprung up overnight between mother and daughter. Eloise, as the girl was named, usually sparkling and vivacious, was now dull and spiritless. Formerly talkative and lovely, she was now silent and depressed."

If Mrs. Blanchard could be accused of being inquisitive, she also was guilty of a warm, sympathetic nature. Looking at the girl, at her mother, then at Walters, she sized up the situation in a flash: While Mrs. Forbes loved Walters, and he loved she, Eloise, too, was in love with him! Now, instead of being constant companions, mother and daughter were rivals, avoiding each other. Meeting only at dinner and in their little stateroom at night, they said little.

Only Walters failed to sense the dramatic change in atmosphere.

Upon another fine evening, Mrs. Blanchard was again enjoying the balmy weather on deck when Eloise joined her. Resting forlornly on the rail, she sighed heavily, remarking upon the calm sea. For some minutes, the older woman watched her carefully, conversing generally. Finally, unable to restrain herself, Mrs. Blanchard asked why she was so sad.

"I cannot tell you, it is too dreadful!" cried Eloise, fleeing tearfully to her cabin, and leaving an anxious Mrs. Blanchard to conclude she and her mother had quarrelled over Walters.

Then the *Consort* was wrecked, and the weeks of suffering commenced. Throughout the ordeal, mother and daughter remained apart, speaking only when necessary.

With HMS *Forward's* arrival had come the harrowing *Florencia* adventure, and the stormy circumnavigation of Vancouver Island. Upon arrival in Victoria, James Wilcox offered the castaways his Royal Hotel. Through the generosity of proprietor Wilcox and citizens, survivors were soon on their feet again. Weeks later, all had continued on their different ways, leaving only Mrs. Forbes, Eloise, and Walters.

The eager mate, who listed money among his abilities, had fulfilled his shipboard promise, replacing the seal ring with a large diamond, and pressed plans for the imminent nuptials. All proceeded smoothly until a month after their arrival in town.

One day, guests at the Royal were startled to hear raised voices from the head of the stairs and, upon looking up, saw Mrs. Forbes and

Eloise arguing. Actually, the girl was speaking softly, apparently holding her mother back. The older woman, rebuffing her angrily, "threw off the hand with an air of petulance, and stepping backward, missed her footing and fell headlong to the foot of the stairs, where she lay motionless, a tiny stream of blood issuing from beneath her head and creeping over the floor like a crimson snake."

Paralyzed by shock, Eloise stood fast as bystanders rushed forward, carrying the unconscious mother to her room. A doctor soon arrived to diagnose a fractured skull — and possibly worse.

Now hysterical, her former coolness toward her mother vanished, Eloise prayed aloud for her "dear mamma." Just then, Walters charged into the room. At the sight of her mother's suitor, Eloise screamed repeatedly, begging those present to send him away.

"But I have done nothing wrong," he protested. "Is it a crime to love and wish to marry your mother? Your mother is a good, true woman and although I can never hope to take the place in her affections of the late Mr. F—"

Then, as bystanders gasped in awe, Eloise shrieked, "The late Mr. Forbes! There is no late Mr. Forbes. My father is still alive!"

As the stunned mariner began to interject that Mrs. Forbes could legally marry upon divorce, Eloise screamed, "My mother and father are not divorced! My mother is a married woman and Father should now be on his way here from Honolulu, for I wrote and told him all about you and Mother as soon as we got here."

Mechanically, Walters pulled the marriage license, obtained that morning, from his tunic. His mouth moved uncontrollably, but no words came, and a sympathetic proprietor Wilcox, placing a hand gently upon his shoulder, whispered: "Here, sir, you had better leave."

Then, as Eloise was led, weeping hysterically, to her room, poor Walters stumbled blindly into the street.

Days after, Mr. Forbes arrived to take his place with Eloise at his wife's side. Slowly, the injured woman recovered. But never a word of her tragic affair was mentioned, Mrs. Forbes stating that her memory "was a blank after the brig sailed from Honolulu."

"It must be the seasickness," she smiled wanly, and the affair was ended.

With her full recovery, the reunited family sailed for Honolulu. As for the crushed John Walters, "he drifted away, and was not heard of again," Mr. Higgins concluded.

Thus ended the real story behind the wreck of the brig *Consort*, over a century ago.

Chapter 5

Torpedoed!

Even the stars seemed reluctant to disturb the dark and stillness of the night of June 19, 1942, remaining hidden in an overcast sky.

The Pacific lay flat and calm, only a wavering streak of phosphorescent white betraying the submarine's presence, as its rapier-like bow parted the waves.

In the conning tower of the undersea raider *I-25*, Commander Meiji Tagami, Imperial Japanese Navy, looked at his watch. It was 2330. Seventy miles to the northeast was Cape Flattery, the massive headland which almost all Pacific Northwest shipping had to pass. But the world was at war and the shipping lanes unfrequented.

For hours Tagami had been running on the surface, the throbbing of his own diesel engines the only sound. Yawning loudly, he shifted the heavy night glasses hanging from his neck and peered into the humid darkness...

A few miles to the north, running without lights, steamed the new 7,126-ton freighter *Fort Camosun*. Built by Victoria Machinery Depot, to the order of the U.S. War Shipping Administration, she was on "bare boat charter" to the British Ministry of War Transport. Now on her maiden voyage, she rode low in the water, holds and deck space crammed with plywood, lead, zinc and other vital materials for the manufacture of munitions.

By midnight, *Camosun* was proceeding through an apparently empty sea, her lookouts scanning the darkness wearily, for they were in protected waters and felt safe enough. Now it was the morning of June 20...

Suddenly a muffled explosion ripped *Camosun's* hull below the bridge, opening No. 2 and No. 3 holds to the sea. Near-naked men, jolted from sleep, stumbled from passageways, yelling, "Torpedo!"

In his radio shack the stunned wireless operator urgently keyed out news of the attack and the ship's position, reporting *Fort Camosun* to be rapidly filling and already starting to settle.

The distress signal was picked up immediately and the Commanding Officer Pacific Coast instructed HMC Corvettes *Quesnel* and *Edmundston*, then in the Strait of Juan de Fuca, to proceed to *Camosun's* assistance. *Quesnel* was returning from convoy duty and *Edmundston* was engaged in anti-submarine patrol off Sheringham Point when each received the order.

As the corvette sped southward, *Camosun* was being shelled by the submarine. Apparently Commander Tagami was dissatisfied with her rate of sinking, and rather than use a second precious torpedo, half-heartedly turned his deck gun on the crippled merchantman.

Calmly directed by her officers, *Camosun's* crew launched lifeboats and pulled away to safety, leaving the ship dead in the water with all power cut off.

The first shell missed, streaking over her bow, but the second, which followed about 30 minutes later, exploded amidships on the starboard side. The sea poured in faster.

HMCS *Quesnel*, Lieutenant John A. Gow commanding, arrived on the scene a little past 0800, to find the battered freighter still afloat. *Quesnel's* asdic immediately detected the *I-25*, which had submerged but was still present, and closed to attack as HMCS *Edmundston*, which had followed close astern, picked up *Camosun's* 31-man crew.

About noon, Lieutenant Raiffe D. Barrett, a veteran sailor of the China coast, and *Edmundston's* commanding officer, took *Camosun* in tow. By this time the sea was reaching for her railings, her boilers were cold and she had no steering gear. Two hours later, Lieutenant Barrett was forced to slip the towline, very little progress having been made.

By late afternoon, contact with the submarine had been lost, but *Camosun* remained afloat, wallowing ponderously in a rising sea. Barrett again pulled alongside and sent aboard a party to jettison some of the deck cargo of lumber and to pump out the holds. But the pumps would not draw and he had to abandon this attempt also.

Just before he cast off, the powerful Vancouver Tug *Dauntless* arrived from Gray's Harbor and took *Camosun* in tow. HMC Corvette *Vancouver*, Lieutenant Percival F.M. De Freitas, in company of the U.S. Armed Yacht *Y-994*, also reached the scene to strengthen the anti-submarine cover.

Midnight came with *Fort Camosun* yawing so much at her cable that this tow had to be dropped too. At 0230 the next morning, the American tugs *Henry Foss*, of Tacoma, and USS *Tatnuck* arrived. By dawn all three had again taken *Camosun* in charge, assisted by the newly-arrived tug *Salvage Queen*, out of Victoria.

The night of June 21-22 passed with the flotilla still struggling with its unruly ward. Again *Camosun* was yawing badly and it was noticed that she was settling deeper in the water.

After passing Cape Flattery she grew even more unmanageable and it was decided to take her into Neah Bay. This necessitated the four tugs securing themselves alongside the freighter, the operation being controlled from aboard the *Camosun* by Chief Skipper Leighton Evans, RCNR, of HMCS *Quesnel*.

After more exhausting hours of struggle, *Camosun* was at last anchored in seven fathoms, part of her resting on the bottom. By this time her foredeck was awash and her stern barely above water.

Leaving the hulk to *Salvage Queen* and HMCS *Edmundston*, HMCS *Quesnel* returned the *Camosun's* crew to Esquimalt, as the other vessels returned to port.

Later HMCS *Nenamook* reached Neah Bay with a naval diver, as a salvage expert and a second diver were flown to the scene. While *Edmundston* patrolled off the bay, the salvors began work. It was then learned that the plywood which comprised most of her cargo had been responsible for keeping her afloat.

On the morning of June 24, *Camosun* was ready for towing, and another tug, *Canadian National No. 2*, joined the team.

With both towboats straining at their lines, *Fort Camosun* was soon underway, but once more began yawing heavily. Lieutenant Barrett then secured *Edmundston* alongside to steer, enabling the tugs to make four knots through the Strait of Juan de Fuca. The following afternoon, *Camosun* was safely anchored in Esquimalt Harbor.

Eventually repaired, *Fort Camosun* survived the war and as late as 1959 was still afloat and operated by the U.S. Department of Commerce.

Camosun's torpedoing off Cape Flattery by the Japanese submarine *I-25*, or *I-26* (it is believed it was Commander Tagami's *I-25*, although this is not definite), was the first of only two such incidents on this coast throughout the Second World War.

On the same night, June 20, while Canadian warships had endeavored to save the stricken freighter, a Japanese submarine surfaced about two miles off Estevan Point, on Vancouver Island's west coast. She fired approximately 25 shells at the lighthouse there but beyond scaring the residents, little damage was inflicted. The event was never repeated.

Chapter 6

Grappler's *Fateful Voyage*

Even to a coast which has known disaster at sea from the beginning, the *Grappler* tragedy ranks as one of the all-time worst.

Sudden storms, treacherous currents, uncharted reefs, marauding Indians...many were the dangers which stalked mariners a century ago. Yet another, greater, threat accompanied every voyage in that perilous age of sail and steam—fire. Hand pumps and courage were pathetic defence against this killer.

There was no warning of the coming holocaust when little steamer *Grappler* cleared Victoria for the last time, early in the evening of Saturday, April 28, 1883. To Captain John F. Jagers, it was another routine run. No stranger to B.C. waters, the 32-year-old German's log included a long stint as mate and master of the famous HBC steamer, *Beaver.*

Grappler was no newcomer, either. All of 37 years, she was a maritime pioneer. Built during the Crimean War, the 230-tonner accompanied sister gunboat, HMS *Forward,* to Esquimalt in 1860. After nine hectic years as watchdogs—accomplishing every duty from that of coast guard to hunting whisky peddlers to capturing Indian murderers—the aging twins were sold at public auction. *Forward* went on to meet violent death far to the south, *Grappler* in her home seas.

Bursting with cannery supplies, gunpowder and 100 passengers, mainly Chinese cannery workers, *Grappler* put in at Departure Bay for 40 tons of coal. Unloading 50 kegs of powder at Nanaimo Sunday afternoon (a fortunate schedule in light of later events), she continued northward on the last lap of her fateful voyage. About 4 p.m., Captain Jagers acquired the services of pilot Sidney Franklyn from the inbound steam schooner, *Grace.*

By 10 o'clock that night, Duncan Bay was astern, the weather mild, the seas calm. As passengers squirmed restlessly in their cramped quarters, Engineer William Steele was anxiously sniffing about his ancient boiler. Seconds later, he hissed in Jagers' ear: "Captain, there's a fire in the for'ard hold!"

Jagers instantly summoned Mate John Smith from his berth and informed him of the danger. "For God's sake, say nothing about it to the passengers—keep it quiet!" replied the first officer, then streaked below.

He ordered two Indian firemen to clear the coal from 'tweendecks, but as the smoke increased with every shovelful, Smith realized the fire was well advanced. Shouting for the hatches to be sealed, he and a deckhand wrestled a hose into position. On the bridge, Captain Jagers gave four sharp blasts from his whistle in the hopes of alerting anyone ashore, and told Franklyn to put about for Duncan Bay.

Passenger David Brown was retiring when he "heard hurried trampling and thinking all was not right went forward and saw smoke and smouldering fire outside and back of the furnace.

"I immediately returned to where my uncle, H. McClusky, was asleep and said in a low voice: 'Get up at once, the ship is on fire, telling him at the same time not to alarm the other passengers. The injunction was, however, unnecessary, for all in a moment, as it seemed, the vessel became a mass of flames and then ensued a scene which beggars description."

Another passenger, Captain John McCallister, was shipping four skiffs to his upcoast cannery. Aroused by shouts as flames swept the engineroom, he hurried below to offer his services. Engineer Steele was desperately trying to couple a hose. Racing topside, McAllister shouted at the panic-stricken passengers pouring from their cabins to form a bucket brigade. It was no use. The terrified Chinese could think only of reaching the lifeboats—with a total capacity of 22 persons.

By now *Grappler's* feverish decks were grey with smoke. Seeing he had little hope of launching the mobbed lifeboats, McAllister ran aft to clear his fishing skiffs. Lungs heaving in the acrid fumes, as *Grappler's* abandoned engines thundered at full speed, the mariner could loose only one craft, which he tumbled over the stern, then leaped after it. By the time he pulled himself over the gunwhale, a white man and a Chinese had already boarded.

Ears ringing with the shrieks of the dying, McAllister looked about for oars. There were none. Undismayed, he salvaged a broom and a bamboo cane from the floating debris and began sculling his unwieldly skiff toward Valdez Island. Within minutes, his hands were raw, but the heroic canner struggled on. Suddenly, the alarmed expressions of his passengers made him wheel about.

Blazing from end to end, steering gone, *Grappler* had reversed course and was charging down on them at full speed! The galloping inferno lunged at the skiff, then arched away. They were safe, for the moment. As she flew by, like some hideous, flaming bird, singeing them with her fiery breath, several passengers saw their last chance and leaped over the side. Painfully ferrying his craft back and forth, McAllister rescued "five or six men...and two or three Chinamen."

One Chinese had been supporting himself on a plank, which McAllister split in two for paddles, handing them to his strongest passenger.

"In the meantime," said the *Colonist,* "the steamer kept going backwards and forwards in an erratic manner, the passengers shrieking and yelling for assistance and the flames spreading rapidly over the vessel."

Landing his survivors on Valdez Island, McAllister paddled to where *Grappler* had made her last turn, picking up a "Chinaman, a Siwash, Steele, the engineer, and several other white men, making about a boatload... Although...loathe to go ashore from the shrieks which were being incessantly given from those around, discretion compelled him, his boat being full, to put to shore again."

By now, almost exhausted, hands blistered and bleeding, McAllister "had terrible hard work to land. Being exceedingly close to the (Seymour) Narrows and the tide increasing rapidly, he did not consider it safe to venture out again, but lit a fire to warm those who were half dead with the cold, some having been upwards of an hour in the water."

Most dramatic account of that horror-filled April night is that of passenger David Brown. Upon rousing his uncle, named McClusky, they hastened on deck. "Men, some of them half-dressed," Brown recounted, "running frantically to and fro half bereft of reason, calling on others to save them, the cries of the horrified Chinamen adding to the fearful confusion...!

"As fast as a boat was lowered men jumped down into it — whites, Chinese, Indians — the coolies actually attempting to save their property, throwing clothing and bags of rice into the boats which capsized almost as soon as they were lowered. I could see there was no chance of saving my life by these means and took a set of steps, made it fast to a line, and threw it overboard, allowing it to tow alongside. When I saw the vessel had become unmanageable and that there was no possibility or running her ashore I dropped overboard, cast off the line and supported by the steps was rapidly borne away with the current."

He had not been in the water long when he spotted one of McAllister's skiffs, drifting keel up, and managed to "scramble on top of it, but had great difficulty in keeping there owing to the boat turning and tumbling in the numerous eddies." Nearby Ripple Rock's lethal rips curned his precarious float "among some Chinamen who were supporting themselves with various articles. Two or three grabbed my legs and as I felt my hold slackening I exerted all my strength and managed to free myself."

He "had scarcely done so when I saw a white man clinging to a small plank and called to him, as he appeared nearly exhausted, to keep up a little longer and was shortly enabled to assist him on the boat.

"I had long before this lost sight of the ill-fated *Grappler* but my companion and I kept up our spirits till we heard the roar of rapids and felt the increased strength of the current. We were spun round and round in the whirlpools, sometimes under the water and sometimes above, but held on like grim death. At last, about an hour after sunrise (they had been adrift for more than eight torturous hours) we drifted ashore on an island and were found in the afternoon by a couple of Indians in a canoe, who took us to a camp of loggers."

Upon being awakened by his nephew, Henry McClusky dressed and sped topside, where he became separated from Brown in the chaos. Seeing a group of whites axing down one of the ship's yards, to serve as a float, he helped them muscle it to the rail. But the timber was too heavy; in the frantic twilight it slipped overside and vanished astern. At this setback, McClusky decided to chance the water and jumped. By extreme good fortune, *Grappler's* wake swept him right alongside the runaway spar. Clinging to the pole, he watched *Grappler* "disappear round a point of land, a perfect sheet of flame and oh! how my heart bled for them, knowing there were none near to save."

Finally he was picked up by McAllister and taken ashore, where he saw the dying steamer return with the tide, "burnt nearly to the water's edge and sink almost in the same place where she had been when the fire started."

One elderly passenger, Robert K. Hall of Vallejo, Calif., had a close call. He had helped Captain McAllister launch his skiff, then leaped to the assistance of some deckhands trying to lower a starboard lifeboat. But the after tackle fouled, allowing the boat to swing by its stern. Jumping into the almost vertical craft, Hall and company clutched the seats as a volunteer hacked at the tackle with a knife.

When the rope parted, the boat somersaulted into the sea, pitching its nine occupants in every direction. As Hall, desperate, decided to try swimming ashore, all about him "the spectacle presented was a most dreadful one, heightened by the shrieks of the drowning Chinamen."

He was almost exhausted and about to give up when Mate John Smith and three others found him. Their boat was half-submerged, but Hall gripped its stern until another passenger, Edward Lane, rescued him in one of the ship's boats, taking him ashore.

The escape of passenger Henry Halenkamp was miraculous. When the lifeboat he had helped launch capsized under the weight of too many bodies, Halenkamp was dragged under. Although it was but seconds, it seemed an eternity that he remained under, unable to surface. He was "full of salt water and my senses were beginning to leave me" when "some object striking the boat caused her, though full of water, to right herself." He gratefully clambered aboard with four others, to be rescued by some of *Grappler's* crew.

Others told dramatic and heartrending tales of escape. Passenger John Cardano broke an arm when his boat capsized upon launching. He had to use his remaining fist to punch his way into one of McAllister's skiffs, occupied by two panicky Chinese. Sailor Mike Conlin and five comrades were trapped in the forecastle by flames. One managed to beat down a hatch—with his head—and reach deck, Conlin at his heels. But the three others were burned alive.

Like Captain McAllister, Captain Jagers, First Officer Smith and Pilot Franklyn, who remained at his blazing post in a vain attempt to steer the ship, Conlin was a hero. When *Grappler* had passed within a half-mile of shore, someone had cried: "For God's sake, somebody get a line ashore!" Conlin volunteered.

His lonely swim became a nightmare. Two hundred feet from the ship, he looked back. At that instant, some of "the poor wretches who were being burned" fastened themselves to his hawser. Lest he be pulled under, cursing and sobbing violently, the courageous seaman let go of the rope. Finally struggling ashore, he collapsed on the beach. It was four frigid hours before Captain McAllister found him and hustled him to a fire.

But even hell must know an end. By morning it was over, and valiant McAllister rowed to Nanaimo for help. When *Grappler*, charred to the waterline, sank, she had claimed almost a hundred lives. The exact figure was not known, as ticket records were inaccurate.

Chapter 7

Tragedy Stalked the Castaways

"A terrible tale of suffering...a coast tragedy without parallel," cried *Colonist* headlines, January 14, 1896.

Although shipwrecks were so frequent as to be almost commonplace off Vancouver Island's treacherous western shore, 70 years ago, the *Janet Cowan's* ordeal is unequalled.

One hundred and eight days out of Cape Town, the *Cowan* raised Cape Flattery light on December 29. For 48 hours Captain Thompson vainly tried to stand off under a bitter sou'wester which steadily beat his lightly-laden, 2,497-ton ship into Barkley Sound. While seeking shelter in the driving blizzard, *Janet Cowan* ground into jagged rocks off Carmanah Pount. It was 2 a.m., December 31, 1895.

Above the roar of wind, wave and buckling plates, the crew debated their chances. The windjammer was rapidly breaking up just 80 yards from shore.

It might have been 80 miles—no lifeboat could survive that frenzied surf.

"But there was a hero equal to the occasion, as there is in nearly all such calamities, and he stepped to the front." Able Seaman J. Chamberlain offered to swim to shore with a lifeline.

"It's suicide!" shouted Captain Thompson. As the young Englishman tore off his clothes, his frightened comrades erupted in cheers, then fell silent. Their lives rested upon a slight youth's courage—a boy against the Pacific Ocean. He did not have a chance.

Securing the line about his neck, Chamberlain paused, took a last look about his ship, the leaped into the sea. Naked and alone, he vanished in the pounding surf. Moments later, even the most optimistic had given him up for dead.

But Chamberlain was alive—barely. Although a strong swimmer, the threshing currents were pulling him under. Blue from the overpowering cold, bleeding from a hundred cuts after being raked across razor-sharp reefs, he struggled on. Somehow he kept his head above water, desperately gasping for air. He was blinded by salt spray, although he did not have to worry about direction as the breakers would sweep him ashore. If only he could keep his head up just a little longer...

Suddenly his lashing feet struck something solid. Land! Surging ahead with his last strength, he was drawn back, then held fast. He was trapped.

Hours passed. Anxiously, those aboard the ship waited for a jerk on the line. But no signal came. Nothing could be seen in the raging blackness. Chamberlain was gone.

They could not know his lifeline had tangled on the bottom, that, too weak to free it, he must save himself—if he could. Wooden fingers tore frantically at the noose, finally slipped it off. Dragging himself forward, Chamberlain torturously crawled into a hollow log for warmth. In the darkness, he did not realize he had not reached shore but a reef some distance away. A reef which would be awash at high tide.

At last the wind slackened enough to allow volunteers to launch a boat and, landing on Chamberlain's tiny ledge, they found their courageous shipmate and hustled him into dry clothing. He was paralyzed after his four-hour ordeal.

Securing a hawser to the ship, the boatmen rigged a breeches-buoy. Soon all of *Janet Cowan's* crew had reached the temporary safety of the ledge. But, again, they were prisoners. They still were a long way from the beach, a wild surf between, and the tide was coming in. Soon their island would be submerged.

Again, a hero answered the call. This anonymous savior struggled ashore, where he set up the lifeline from a rocky bluff. One at a time, the 29 shipwrecked mariners rode the bosun's chair to safety. Midway, Captain Thompson's benumbed fingers lost their grip, plunging him toward the sea when his feet hooked in the ropes and, dangling headlong over the rocks, he was hauled ashore.

Sheltering in the trees, they built a fire. Nine men immediately began searching the area, eventually stumbling upon the Carmanah Point-Cape Beal telegraph line. Following it in the dark, they came upon a small cabin a mile down the beach and moved in.

"The balance of the crew," reported the *Colonist*, "passed the night as best they could, some of them getting their feet frostbitten. The fire...is all that kept them alive.

"Early the next morning several of the men were sent aboard the ship, which still remained in an upright position, and brought back canvas, provisions, ship's valuables and, in fact, everything moveable. While rummaging about the vessel for stores, First Mate Legall fell down a scuttle hole and broke his leg. He was taken ashore, lashed to the (bosun's) chair, and carried to the camp in the woods."

Tragedy continued to stalk the castaways. That afternoon, having ransacked the ship, Second Mate John Howell and apprentices Walter Logan and William T. Steele headed back to shore. Without warning, their fragile boat capsized in the towering breakers. Days later, their bodies could be seen "being beaten against the rocks..."

On the second morning Captain Thompson divided his men into squads, having them scour the snowbound beach in opposite directions. He was confident there was some form of settlement nearby, as evidenced by the telegraph line and cabin. He could not know there was only Carmanah lighthouse, four miles to the west, and its keeper could not see *Janet Cowan* from his perch. The telegraph was no help as the same storm which had wrecked their ship had broken the line in a dozen places. Their only hope was a passing ship or Indian fisherman.

The weary seamen returned to camp with grim reports. Other than the shack, they had found not a sign of human life. Fever-wracked Thompson ordered them out the next day. And the next. But to no avail. They were alone.

By now Thompson and several hands were feeling the effects of exposure and exhaustion. Amazingly, young Chamberlain had not only recovered from his daring swim but was one of the most active. Even when both feet froze, he continued hobbling about, nursing the others.

The men constructed a crude tent of sail canvas as a hospital for Captain Thompson, Mate Legall, the cook and three seamen. But without medical supplies, there was little Chamberlain and Steward Taylor could do.

On the fifth day of their stranding, Thompson died.

The loss of their master was a severe blow to the men. Thompson had kept them active and cheerful. With the first mate injured, the second officer drowned, the crew began to disintegrate. Nights were bitterly cold, the days empty. There was little to do, just one thing to talk about—rescue. They could only wait. And pray.

On the sixth day, the cook and two others died. The engineer's last hours were hellish; raving violently, he had to be forcibly restrained until death ended his torment.

The final misfortune—which convinced all that "the fates were against them"—came when the camp was deserted, all but Mate Legall and seaman Hunt vainly searching the empty beaches for help. In their makeshift hospital, Legall was lashed to a chair, Hunt rolled in a blanket on the earth floor. Both were helpless. Suddenly Legall

41

identified an odor he had noticed earlier — smoke.

"Hunt, the tent's burning!"

Unable to stand, Legall frantically yelled for rescue. There was no one to hear. Hunt could not move. Then Legall's casting eyes fell upon a rifle near the door. If he could just...reach it...his fingers clawed empty space. Savagely rocking his chair from side to side, the desperate officer inched toward the weapon. The chair tipped, spinning him onto his face in the dirt. But he had the gun.

Two shots brought the others running. The snow-shrouded canvas had not burned easily, although flames were reaching for Hunt when help arrived.

This incident drained the last ounce of hope and, to a man, they sank into a pit of despondency. In complete silence, sprawled about the fire, they waited; for death or rescue, they no longer cared which.

Days passed, the men stirring only to keep the fire alight or eat. Each morning, those in the line shack hiked to camp for food and implored their companions to return with them. But Legall and Hunt could not be moved. Even in their despair, the seamen would not consider abandoning their ailing shipmates.

They did not know that help was coming...

Enroute to Alberni, Commodore John Irving had spotted *Janet Cowan*, still upright, sails set, from the bridge of his sidewheeler, *Princess Louise*. Unable to put ashore in the running sea and gathering darkness, Irving proceeded to port and telegraphed Victoria authorities. Returning the following day, Irving still could not make a landing.

Fortunately, upon the news, Captain J.B. Libby of Puget Sound Tugboat Company had immediately dispatched the tugs *Pioneer* and *Holyoke*. But it was a full three days after Irving's sighting that a third company craft, *Tyee*, succeeded in landing men.

"A sight met their gaze that will not be forgotten for years to come. Seated about a fire on pieces of wood and on the ground were 13 men, all wearing an expression of utter helplessness and misery. At the sight of *Tyee's* men the scene was transformed into one of hope and hilarious joy. The castaways jumped to their feet and embraced their rescuers."

Mate Hall of the Seattle tugboat described the memorable experience:

"Captain Gove thought it best to make an attempt to land in the tug's small boats, so I took several men, and Chief Hawkins took several, and we started.

"By good hard pulling, we soon got alongside the ship and then passed under her bow. Once on the port side the water was comparatively quiet and we had but little trouble in making a landing. There was a rope stretched from the ship's side to the shore, so we knew that the crew was safe. After making a landing we climbed up a rope ladder that led to the top of a bluff which we could not see from the other side of the ship, and came upon the crew in a tent at the top.

"They were mighty glad to see us, I tell you. They wanted us to take them on board the tug right away. We assured them that they would be looked out for, and then started to look around for ourselves. They told us a terrible story of how they had suffered and what they had gone through with, and it broke me all up. When they finished with the story we started into the woods to look for the bodies of the captain and the other men that had died from the cold and privations, intending to bury them, but we could not find them. Why, these poor chaps didn't have life enough to tell us where the place was."

Days later, those from the cabin were in Victoria. It would be months before the bodies of Captain Thompson and the others could be recovered and buried in Ross Bay Cemetery.

Poor *Janet Cowan* had been the victim of ignorance. Ignorance which cost seven lives and a 10-day nightmare for 22 others. Had Captain Thompson not been a stranger to this deadly coast, he would have crowded on sail and continued up the strait, rather than retreating to seaward. Then, once stranded, the crew should have remained aboard – a fact they could not foretell as it seemed that the *Cowan* would break up immediately. Had they stayed on the ship, in comparative comfort, it is unlikely any lives would have been lost.

Chapter 8

Flight of the Kaare II

A daring little ship that defied German guns and the stormy North Atlantic during the Second World War, to vanish in the moody Pacific a quarter of a century after, provides one of the Northwest's most intriguing marine mysteries.

The 65-foot halibut boat *Kaare II* disappeared in October, 1963, in gale-swept Hecate Strait with her six-man crew. As a vast armada of vessels and aircraft searched for the missing vessel, newspapers recalled her courageous flight from Nazi-occupied Norway, 23 years before.

For years Ottar Novik and brothers Hans, Alfred, Hoken, Ove and Haftan had sailed *Kaare II* out of Christiansun, fishing in the cold waters off their homeland as they had all their lives. But war brought an end to this arduous, satisfying existence. With the fall of Norway, German occupation forces directed every aspect of Norwegian life. Among those to feel the invaders' iron rule were the fishing Noviks. No longer could they harvest the fertile grounds they had known so long. German naval officers, perhaps for strategic or security reasons, ordered the fishing fleet "elsewhere, often to barren grounds," wrote George Nicholson.

Like their compatriots, the Noviks' catch "was frequently commandeered by German gunboats with little or no compensation and their gear was often damaged or destroyed by mines and submarines."

Then there were searches by patrol boats after the bullion which vessels of the Norwegian Underground were smuggling out to British warships, to return with guns, ammunition and instructions of sabotage.

Ashore, it was worse. Families of fishermen lived in constant terror, aware they were continually watched. In this manner the Germans held them, in effect, hostages for the scheduled return of the menfolk. Also, to again quote Mr. Nicholson, "trade with the outside world was almost entirely cut off; food was scarce and fear of drunken soldiers made living conditions for families intolerable. The presence of possible Quislings didn't help matters."

Finally came the day when Ottar Novik, owner and master of the *Kaare II*, and his brothers decided they had no choice but to take a desperate gamble. The future held the strong possibility of losing their boat, imprisonment, or, perhaps, worse. Thus it was they decided to flee to Canada.

Then came weeks of clandestine meetings, planning and rehearsing. Ottar co-ordinated the secret preparations of his brothers, their wives and children. All told, 23 Noviks and in-laws were involved. Finally a plan was decided upon and the great adventure was begun.

In following weeks, *Kaare II* went about her business with an air of complete innocence. German directives were obeyed to the letter; nothing must arouse suspicion. At sea, she fished precisely where told, yielded to all orders of patrol craft and returned to port on schedule.

Her men even became friendly with crews of the shore batteries guarding the harbor entrance. Where once the Norwegians passed in stony silence, eyes straight ahead, now they slowed to hail the sentries, "sometimes even calling them by name and sometimes stopping to give them a few fish."

Finally, the fateful morning of June 9, 1940, arrived. As she had so many times before, with only her usual ration of fuel, *Kaare II* slipped her moorings and headed to sea. In the pilothouse and on deck, Ottar Novik and his brothers waved gaily to the shore batteries, then received the signal to leave harbor. Little diesel purring, *Kaare II* left her homeport forever.

At their usual posts were Ottar, Hans, Alfred, Hoken, Ove and Haftan. Below, in her dark, damp and supposedly empty holds were 17 frightened souls: the Novik women, brothers-in-law Ingvor and Peter Engvik, "their wives, six children ranging in age from 13 to three years, and a seven-month-old baby."

The previous night had been one of sheer terror, when, "one by one, past unsuspecting sentries, they were smuggled aboard.

"The women folk were disguised as men and the children bundled into dunnage bags. Only such baggage as could be taken aboard without creating suspicion was brought along. The remainder of their household belongings were left behind. Their relatives dared not touch their abandoned possessions for fear of being implicated. Lights were left burning in their homes."

At sea, the fear remained. German planes and submarines ruled the Norwegian Sea. They must continue their roles as innocent fishermen. The women and children were kept below in the stuffy cabins and holds, to keep them from sight of fellow fishermen and patrol boats. Whenever a German aircraft passed over, the Noviks fished; as soon as the enemy flew on, they resumed course.

Then, during the second night at sea—disaster. *Kaare II* was proceeding through the black, rolling sea when her helmsman suddenly spotted a large object looming up dead ahead. Throwing the helm hard over, *Kaare II* barely missed the alien: a U-boat. In terror, her 23 souls awaited the inevitable challenge and search. Seconds passed. A minute. Two. Still the German did not challenge; even seemed unaware of their presence. *Kaare II* passed on into the night and safety.

Days later, their miraculous luck seemed to have ended when a German plane swept out of the clouds. Circling the little ship, the German scanned her decks, then roared down to attack, machineguns blazing. Instantly, Ottar stopped his engine and *Kaare* wallowed in the swells. And once again her frightened company awaited imminent doom. And once again their amazing fortune held. The aircraft buzzed them a last time then flew off. They were alone once more.

Five days out, off the Faeroe Islands of Denmark, they encountered another ship. This time there was no agonizing wait for imminent capture. The stranger was a British destroyer, which escorted her to port to refuel. The Noviks' friends in the resistance had sent word ahead of their odyssey.

Two weeks later, *Kaare II* began the 10-day voyage to St. John's, Newfoundland. Except for bad weather, the passage was uneventful. This time, the only ships met were friendly. The Noviks then continued on to Nova Scotia, where they fished for cod for several months. Electing to begin anew in British Columbia, eight members of the seagoing families sailed down the east coast of the United States, through the Panama Canal, then headed north as the remainder crossed Canada by train. On April 28, 1941, battered *Kaare II* moored in Vancouver, the port which was to be her home for 22 years.

When she steamed proudly into harbor, the Norwegian flag snapping proudly at her stern, her beaming crew happily showed one and all their memento of a daring voyage which, but for a miracle, would have ended in disaster: In the keel of her port dinghy was a hole the size of a Novik fist—only damage caused when the Nazi plane strafed her months before in the Norwegian Sea.

The brothers went cod and halibut fishing, then Ottar sold out to Haftan, building, with Alfred and Hans, the big seiner *Kaare*, to engage in salmon, halibut and herring fishing.

October 29, 1963, *Kaare II* was again making headlines. This time, under command of another owner, Captain Anfelt Antonsen, Jr., his younger brother John and a four-man crew, *Kaare II*'s incredible luck had at last been exhausted. At first there was hope she had anchored

46

in an isolated cove to escape a series of gales which had lashed Hecate Strait that month. Among those inclined to think she was safe was one of the Noviks, who said: "I can't see her having gone down in a storm. We ran a lot of weather in the years when we had her. If she's gone down, she must have struck a reef."

Air-Sea Rescue mounted an intensive search by ships and planes in the following days. But each passing hour brought the realization that gallant *Kaare II* had fought her last battle. The missing captain's father, Anfelt Antonsen, Sr., remained hopeful until the end. Finally, two plastic floats, positively identified as belonging to the missing heroine, were found on a bleak Alaskan shore.

The senior Antonsen and another son, Steinar, had been fishing in the same area that last day. "One wave could have done it," the old fisherman surmised. "It was a very hard blow that night. I was not far from it...there was a hard blow. The sea and the wind have taken bigger and stronger boats than she was. She was taken by wind and a big sea. I figure it this way: She had no chance to send an SOS. She was well equipped with radio and two sounders.

"Even when they were in port the boys used to give us a call every day. The wave must have hit so quickly they didn't have a chance to call." Sadly, he concluded, "I don't believe they are alive. The search was so big. When you think of the many aircraft and boats searching...they covered everything."

Asked if he would continue fishing, the 62-year-old Norwegian replied, "Fishing is in my blood. It's a tough life, but when it's in your blood you love it."

Early in November of 1968, police investigated wreckage found 45 miles south of Prince Rupert. Three days later Steinar Antonsen indentified the shattered white and grey stern section as the remains of *Kaare II*. The courageous little halibut boat which had braved German guns and Atlantic gales had succumbed, a quarter-century later, to a Pacific storm.

Chapter 9

Deadly Grip of Race Caught Poor Nannette

Ships foundered and men died; it happened so often in the lethal infancy of navigation along British Columbia's treacherous shores that Victoria seemed to be in an almost constant state of mourning. But the loss of the bark *Nannette*, December 23, 1860, ironically provided the city its "gayest" tragedy ever.

For decades after, pioneers fondly remembered poor *Nannette* — the shipwreck that was!

Three-year-old *Nannette*, 385 tons, had cleared London June 30, bound for Victoria with a general cargo valued at $165,000. One hundred and seventy-five days, and 16,000 miles later — within 11 miles of her destination — *Nannette* was caught in the Race's deadly grip, the surging current drawing her ever nearer the waiting rocks. "An old and experienced navigator," Captain Main's misfortune was attributed to "the occurrence of a succession of unfortituous circumstances, against which no seaman could guard."

One of these "unfortituous circumstances" had been Main's dysentery, which confined him to bed less than a month out of Liverpool, compelling Mate William McCulloch to take command for the remainder of the six-month voyage. McCulloch gave a vivid account of the *Nannette*'s final hours:

"About 6 o'clock on Saturday evening, while in the Straits, supposing the ship to be about three miles from the American side, and opposite Race Rocks, shortened sail and hove to. It was thick at the time and we could not see the Rocks; headed northwestward, and supposed that she would drift as far as the mouth of the harbor by the morning with the tide.

"At 8 o'clock," he continued, "saw a light bearing N. by W. ½ W.

(Esquimalt Light); could not find the light marked on the chart. At 8½ o'clock it cleared somewhat, and then saw the point of Race Rocks for the first time, but no light. Called all hands on deck, as we found the ship was in a counter-current, and drifting at the rate of seven knots toward the shore. We made all possible sail, but there was nearly a calm at the time and the sails were of no avail. Kept a hand in the chains all the time and found no bottom at 75 fathoms."

By midnight, helpless *Nannette* was "within 400 yards of the rocks; sounded shortly after in 17 fathoms and continued shoaling our water to seven fathoms when we let go anchor and paid out 45 fathoms of cable. We then hailed the lighthouse, and receiving an answer lowered our gig and went ashore. Shortly after, returned on board bringing all the assistance we could get.

"It being flood at the time, we made all sail and manned the windlass, intending to follow the advice of the men from the Rock (who knew the currents) and if we could do no better pass between the Rock and the Twin Islands."

By then a light wind was blowing from the north and McCulloch turned his ship east northeast, toward the American side. But as soon as the anchor pulled free, the bark again began drifting and struck bottom — hard.

"We immediately let go the halliards," said McCulloch, "and on sounding two pumps, found the ship making water. Got the boats out and by that time found seven feet of water in the hold. We then put four of the crew, who were sick, with some of their clothes, in the boats... Although we had one of the shore men in each boat to point out the landing place, were unable to land owing to the heavy swell. The lighthouse boat was finally swamped in attempting to make shore and the ship's boats remained under the lee of the vessel all night."

McCulloch, the second mate and the crewmen remained aboard to save the ship's instruments and papers, finally abandoning her at 5 a.m. Now the sea was up to her main deck, the *Nannette* canted hard to port and they had to wade across her flooded deck to their boat in water waist deep.

With daylight, the boats succeeded in landing on the Rock, *Nannette*'s sick, including Captain Main, receiving "every attention" from construction workers.

"(HMS) *Grappler* came down about 9 o'clock... When I left the wreck at 11 o'clock this morning, she was totally submerged — the only things to be seen being her spars, davits and bowsprit cap. She will, I fear, prove a total loss, although some of the lighter goods may be picked up when she goes to pieces. The captain did all in his power to save the ship and the crew behaved like men."

Nannette had been victim of McCulloch's ignorance of local waters. Race Rocks Light was then in the last stages of construction, not beaming her first friendly warning until three nights later. The light McCulloch had seen but not found on his chart had been Fisgard Island, just built. Regardless of the cause, *Nannette* was gone. Then began a months-long melee, the likes of which Victoria had not known since the first riproaring days of '58 when the cry "Gold" had swept the colonies. The pages of the *Colonist* of this period form a calendar of comedy; a riot of confusion which reeled from the depths of tragedy to the heights of hilarity.

It began seriously enough, December 26, when the Hudson's Bay Company steamer *Otter* began salvage operations by cutting away the *Nannette*'s rigging. Relieved of this weight, the hulk heeled over, raising one flank above water at low tide. Rigging a windlass, salvors worked day and night to raise 15 casks of ale and several packages of gunpowder.

Two-thirds of the cargo, consigned to Messrs. Stamp & Company, and the HBC, was insured; the balance, $45,000, was on consignment to smaller merchants who were not covered. For them and insurance underwriters who had claimed the wreck, it was no laughing matter.

The next day a plunger brought a quantity of salvaged goods to Victoria, mostly in the form of cases of Old Tom gin. Under command of wreckmaster Captain John M. Thain, salvors cut away *Nannette*'s upper deck to reach her precious holds. The schooner *Mary Ann* was expected to dock shortly with more recovered goods.

December 28, the schooner *Harriot* recovered eight tons of goods, consisting of blankets, clothing, gin, ale... Bales of drygoods were opened on the HBC wharf and their contents "hung out to dry on the long railing at the rear of the warehouse, causing the establishment to resemble...an immense laundry."

Harriot's master said that, when he had left Race Rocks the previous evening, more than a hundred men in small craft were eagerly grappling in the depths with boat hooks and tongs.

"The scene among the wreckers is said to baffle description. Disputes as to the possession of packages fished up are constantly taking place, and not a few rough and tumble fights have taken place. Everyone seems to be working on his own hook, and in every case demands salvage for what he brings up."

Despite their vehement claims to possession, underwriters dared not outlaw freelance salvage efforts. With the first storm *Nannette* would probably slip from her perch into depths beyond recovery. Wreckmaster Thain chose instead to allow the free-for-all to continue, policing the scene with special constables and 50 Royal Navy seamen, whose duty it was to collect all recovered merchandise, salvors to make claims to the underwriters in Victoria.

By New Year's Day, tons of goods had been salvaged. Auctioneer P.M. Backus advertised a gala sale of thousands of articles, ranging from hoop iron boots to seven "monkey jackets."

Meanwhile, the constables had had their hands full preventing looters from filling their own. Finally Captain E. Hammond King laid charges against two Esquimalt residents, Fabian Mitchell, a grocer, and restaurateur "Philip McEverley" (actually one Phillip Machivelli). King said they had "run down to the wreck in the plunger *White Squall* and having filled her with goods, took the same to Esquimalt and secreted them in their houses." Among the goods in question were 50 pairs of fine Wellington boots.

To date, $30,000 worth of cargo had been salvaged. How much more had vanished into hands of looters was not stated, although Captain King and company had a painful idea.

On January 2, death joined the party when a canoe containing five men, an Indian woman and her 18 month old infant, capsized in a deadly rip off Albert Head. Despite warnings, they had foolishly loaded their frail craft to its gunwhales with pilfered goods. When the canoe tipped, only one man reached land after being in the frigid sea for three hours.

Other salvors had had their problems that day, John T. Little & Company's schooner *Rob Roy* sinking when she became entangled in the wreck's rigging. She was raised without difficulty and towed to port, as auctioneer Backus easily disposed of $10,000 worth of merchandise at public sale. Machivelli and Mitchell were remanded a week.

January 4, Alexander Winning lost $10 for possession of stolen goods, three blankets, as police raided cabins on Humboldt Street, recovering a handcart filled with gin and "other drinkables" which had been purloined from *Nannette*'s holds.

At the wreck, Special Constable Alexander Stenhouse had seized $5,000 in cargo from looters. Despite his and Captain King's strenuous efforts, the *Colonist* reported: "Large quantities of cargo are said to have been taken off by men from this place, the other side, and Fraser River."

The mad scramble continued at Race Rocks, freelancers competing bitterly with salvors; "a great deal of drinking and rowdyism is going on at the wreck, and black eyes and broken noses are quite fashionable there." Captain King and Constable Stenhouse were under no illusions as to where all the liquor was coming from!

Things really began to get exciting when Stenhouse, under King's orders, seized the HBC schooner *Thames*. This vessel had cleared at the Victoria customhouse days earlier, giving her destination as Nanaimo. Once out of harbor, her master had sailed straight to the wreck and commenced grappling for cargo. The *Colonist* gained righteous satisfaction from the incident, noting the constables were treating the prominent company as they had all violators, despite threats of a lawsuit.

Company directors were in the news for another reason. At a second auction of salvaged goods, bidding had been spirited for a sealed case, listed in the catalogue as "contents unknown." The factors, who apparently "knew a thing or two about its inmost recesses," finally secured the prized package for $300. Just what it did contain is not recorded.

Another gambler was not, apparently, as lucky, buying a small iron safe for three times its worth. Eagerly opening it, he found it contained..."just nothing at all."

Three more looters were lightly fined, Mitchell and Machivelli were again remanded. January 9, the unhappy pair again faced the magistrate. Defence counsel pleaded they had salvaged several boatloads as an act of pure unselfishness, fully intending to deliver the cargo to authorities—sometime. He had no answer to Wreckmaster Thain's testimony that a search of the accuseds' homes had turned up missing merchandise in some most unlikely places. They were again remanded until Captain King, ferreting out looters at Sooke, returned.

Underwriters ruefully estimated that one-quarter of *Nanette*'s cargo had been stolen.

When Captain King arrived, he had the schooner *Surprise* in custody, having found her in possession of several blankets. He said another schooner, the *Ino*, had escaped to Barkley Sound with "a large quantity" of stolen goods. *Surprise*'s Captain Hugh McKay was surprised with a fine of $250.

Events became even more entangled when C.B. Young charged entrepreneur Harmon Shirpser, known as "Cheap John," with having defrauded him of a valuable bale of plaid. Young said he bought it at auction as a bale of blankets, selling it as such to Shirpser, later learning of its true contents. The complicated case resulted in Shirpser being committed for trial and business associate Jacob Fried being charged with perjury.

By now the *Colonist* was unhappy with Constable Stenhouse for having released the HBC schooner "very mysteriously," despite her having been caught redhanded, loaded with valuable cargo without a permit, and, according to rumor, heading for Washington Territory when seized. "A great deal has been said during the past seriously affecting the character of the officer in giving up the vessel. We should not like to report what people say, but the *price* has been freely named."

To which an indignant Stenhouse replied by letter that the schooner had been freed by his superiors. He regarded the newspaper's insinuations, he said, with "supreme contempt."

Then it was learned that the schooner *Rebecca*, working under permit, had been cheating the underwriters. For each load she brought into Victoria, her wily master sneaked a second across the line under cover of darkness. When Captain King got wind of her misdeeds, *Rebecca* had escaped to the other side.

The U.S. revenue cutter *Jefferson Davis* captured three boats loaded with stolen cargo.

At another auction, HBC factors bid heavily for a large cask of "some of the finest French brandy ever brought to this colony," paying $208. The thirsty factors then tapped the cask, "when, lo! and behold, it was found to contain naught but salt water — in a pure and unadulterated condition." A shrewd salvor had broached the barrel, filled it with water and skilfully resealed it. The factors were, understandably, "highly indignant."

January 16, Mitchell and Machivelli were committed to trial. The next day the *Jefferson Davis* seized two more boats.

A week later, two Rocky Point men were arrested for possession of stolen goods. Then Captain McAlmond of the Schooner *Rebecca* returned to port, to be arrested by Stenhouse. The Rocky Point wreckers were fined, a third man committed for trial, a fourth remanded and the charge of misrepresentation against Harmon Shirpser dropped. Friend Jacob Fried was subsequently acquitted of perjury.

On February 1 one James Hillborn was acquitted of possession, and the inquiry into *Nannette*'s loss found Mate McCulloch guilty of an error in judgement in accepting the lighthouse workers' advice to weigh anchor.

Seven weeks after her sinking, *Nannette* was sold to Captain James M. Reid for $650. By then most of her cargo had been recovered and illegal salvors had retired from the scene. February 15, she slowly slid from the reef into 15 fathoms, ending salvage operations at last.

The case of Mitchell and Machivelli finally ended with their conviction and sentence of six months. Attorney-General Cary also announced his department's intention to confiscate all goods and chattels in their possesstion as authorized by statute.

In the meantime, Captain King had been accidentally killed while searching for the thieving schooner *Ino* in Barkley Sound. Ironically, she had sailed instead to San Juan, leaving two tons of loot in care of the local Indian chief, "a very honorable and trustworthy man." Arrested, Captain Michael Sullivan was jailed to await trial. Raising bail, he hastened to San Juan, to find a cellmate to whom he had bragged of his deception had beaten him there and tricked the chief into surrendering the booty!

The amazing story of ill-fated *Nannette* finally ended seven months later in a courtroom, with Chief Justice Cameron awarding salvors, still unpaid by underwriters, two-fifths of net proceeds of all auctioned cargo.

Thus the books were at last closed on the strange, sometimes tragic, oftimes hilarious, case of the bark *Nannette* — Victoria's wildest shipwreck ever!

Chapter 10

The Killer That Was Ripple Rock

Probably few of the thousands of pleasure and commercial craft annually plying British Columbia's Inside Passage now have much fear of navigating Seymour Narrows. True, this 2,500-foot channel between Vancouver, Maud and Quadra Islands still is hazardous. But, within recent memory, this was the dreaded lair of the worst marine hazard of the entire West Coast — Ripple Rock.

Removal of the Ripple Rock threat, one of the greatest engineering feats in Canadian history, involved many years, millions of dollars... and several lives.

Prior to the epic blast of April 5, 1958, "Old Rip" was a "submerged, steeply-sided mountain situated approximately in the middle of Seymour Narrows. The bulk...is well below the water's surface at low tide, but two pinnacles situated about 410 feet apart in a north-south line reach upward to menace passing ships. The north peak section is approximately 160 feet wide by 360 feet long and the south peak is approximately 150 feet wide by 200 feet long.

"At low tide the tip of the north peak is only about nine feet below the surface and the south peak is approximately 19 feet down."

The dangers of Ripple Rock were well known to early mariners. An 1886 *B.C. Pilot*, published by the British Admiralty, recommended vessels "enter at or near slack water and keep the eastern shore aboard in order to avoid Ripple Rock. Vessels steaming at the rate of 12 knots have been unable to make headway and even to be set back, while attempting the Narrows during spring tides."

Thought to be first to safely navigate the Narrows, where tidal changes can form 17-mile-an-hour currents, was Captain George Vancouver. But many ships and small craft in following years have not been as lucky.

First victims were the American gunboats USS *Saranac* and *Wachusett*. *Saranac* met her grim end June 15, 1875, when transitting the Narrows, then known as Euclataw Rapids, at an uncontrollable speed of 14 knots. Unable to answer her helm in the giant eddies, *Saranac* was swept over the main peak, which gutted her.

Within minutes, her frightened crew drove the sinking paddle-wheeler ashore. When the last longboat left her buckling sides, she slipped to 60 fathoms, a total loss.

Other ships followed...

Apparently "no complete record of losses has been compiled, but it is estimated (in 1956) that since 1875, some 14 large ships have been lost or severely damaged and that more than 100 smaller vessels, fishing boats, tugs and yachts have been sunk with the loss of approximately 114 lives."

The CPR Princesses *Ena, Maquinna* and *Mary*, the CNR "Princes" *George* and *Rupert*, and the CCGS *William J. Stewart* are among the better known ships to have encountered difficulty here.

Seymour Narrows provided another, perhaps greater, headache: Due to its fierce tides, ships were forced to await slack periods, which occur but twice a day. Consequently ships lined up "like cars on Main Street waiting for the green light. At the right moment they dart through from each end causing a heavy traffic which, in itself, is far from desirable in such a restricted passage.

"The yearly loss to ships thus forced to lie idle for long periods add up to millions of hours with consequent cost in dollars."

First to express interest in removing the infamous Rock came, surprisingly, not from a Canadian agency, but from United States Army engineers. The American cableship *Burnside*, enroute to Alaska, had narrowly escaped being sunk in the formidable Narrows, and the chief of engineers suggested "some understanding might be reached with the Canadian government looking to its removal in the interest of shipping...."

This astute observation eventually reached Ottawa, after passing through American, British and, finally, Canadian channels. The American report then seems to have been "filed" — meaning it has not seen the light of day since.

Unfortunately, Ripple Rock could not be forgotten.

During the next 37 years, Seymour Narrows claimed victim after victim, capsizings, collisions and strandings becoming almost commonplace. One reasonably accurate record of mishaps, 1875-1944, lists 27 ships, smaller craft and barges.

In 1931 the government went as far as having a commission investigate possibilities of removing the menace. At which Victoria and Vancouver engaged in a verbal free-for-all, Vancouver favoring the Rock's removal, Victoria demanding it stay!

The provincial capital's strange argument was an old one, dating back to the days of Confederation: Ripple Rock offered the only natural foundation on which a bridge could be constructed to finally, truly unite Vancouver Island with the rest of the province. As the controversy raged, the issue became one of landlubbers versus mariners. The former favored retention of the Rock until it was possible to build a causeway.

Sailors were equally adamant. The Rock had to go—and what was the matter with these lunatics, wanting to compound the threat by building a bridge on top!

The commission favored the latter, and weighed different proposals as to how to do the job. Five plans were examined, four of which were rejected as being "impracticable, too expensive," or too dangerous. Ironically, the theory termed too expensive was the one ultimately employed, and which proved successful.

The best plan, said the commission, as it was "inexpensive and promising success," was to drill and blast the Rock from a floating platform. The estimated cost: a mere $167,500.

The public again joined the act, forwarding several unique proposals, including a Royal Canadian Navy attack with bombs and torpedoes. Even though years began to pass without any concrete action, the suggestions continued to come. One dreamer, in keeping up with the times, favored dropping an atomic bomb. Which does not sound too impractical today when one recalls that the U.S. government has given serious thought to using "clean" nuclear devices in mammoth engineering projects.

The initial attempt to actually remove, or at least reduce, the bottleneck came in 1942. The new interest in such an ambitious undertaking resulted from the Second World War, then raging; both the Canadian and American governments were anxious to have the vital Inside Passage clear to shipping.

Then all they had to do was convince a contracting firm. When no bids were forthcoming, two companies suggested a "cost plus" arrangement. Awarded the contract, B.C. Bridge and Dredging Company started the monumental task by building a complete working model of Seymour Narrows and its underwater monster, including the floating plant with which they intended to perform the job.

Tests finished, a special 150-foot drilling barge was constructed and towed to the site. Six concrete anchors, some weighing 250 tons each, were sunk in either shore and heavy steel cables run across—no mean achievement in itself. The barge was secured to the cables and held over the Rock, to serve as a platform for drilling operations. The plan was to pepper the underwater mountain with holes, filling them with explosives.

Drilling was about to start when the cables, vibrating uncontrollably in the riptide, "snapped like threads!"

Throughout the summer of 1943, workers struggled desperately to anchor the barge. Despite their every effort, the cables continued to break—roughly one every second day.

Work was suspended for the winter, and it was not until the summer of 1945 that another attempt was made. Again, a barge was to be held over the Rock by cables; cables that were 3,500 feet long and weighed 10 tons apiece. But this time, instead of being submerged, victims of treacherous tides, they were strung overhead. Once again the barge was successfully installed, drilling begun.

Winning this preliminary bout was another remarkable achievement of the contractors.

However, by fall, only a pitiful eight percent of the required holes had been bored—at a cost in excess of $1,000,000. Faced with financial disaster, without any guarantee of success, Ottawa dropped the project. This decision was influenced by the drowning of nine workers when their small boat capsized in the frenzied Narrows.

Another eight years passed, mariners still urging the Rock's removal. In 1953 the National Research Council accepted the challenge. When the herculean task of obtaining ore samples from the seabed was completed, the answer became apparent:

Not only were the rock formations the same encountered every day by miners but, better still, the sea did not leak into the test holes. Thus, tunnelling under the Narrows from Maud Island and up through the Rock itself, which had been suggested—and rejected—25 years earlier, was the solution.

Seven hundred and fifty tons of high explosive would provide Old Rip's farewell.

Work began in 1955, a main shaft more than one-half-mile-long being painstakingly carved from Maud Island. None of the tragedy which had broken the back of the wartime scheme plagued this operation, work progressing smoothly but for labor difficulties.

When miners reached the Rock's base, "raises" were extended upward to each peak. Then "coyote drifts" and "boxhole" entries were carved out of Rip's belly. These would hold the special explosive, Nitramex 2H, two years in the developing specifically for this task. The amount had been increased to 1,375 tons—theoretically sufficient to "raise the 390,000-ton Empire State Building one mile straight up!"

But the blast had to be neat as well as powerful; engineers were "required to sheer off mountains that were underwater and throw the rocks so precisely that no dredging would be necessary. The rock must not only be shattered but must also be aimed to fall into submerged holes in the waterway. To let it fly at random would mean dredging it out again; to let it settle back in the same place would not solve the problem."

Quite an order!

As zero hour neared, the RCMP took extensive precautions. Scientists had determined a danger zone of three-mile radius would be created. This area included a safety margin, but the Mounties carefully checked the entire circle, evacuating 65 persons, their pets and livestock.

This was the easier part of the officers' job, for they knew some individuals would risk "having their heads blown off for the sake of a bird's eye view of the blast."

Dozens of old logging roads and trails were barred. As the momentous event drew close, B.C. Forest Service units supplemented RCMP mobile communication trucks, roadblocks were installed, and five RCMP patrol craft and two RCAF crash boats assumed stations at each entrance to the Narrows. An RCMP plane would be on hand to rush any injured to hospital.

But the Mounties' greatest headache promised to be a record traffic jam on the Island Highway near Campbell River. Newspapers, radio and television had given the project such immense publicity that it was expected many would seek front-row seats. However, this problem was solved by using the same news media: An announcement pointed out that the blast could be delayed by adverse weather and the public would find it much more comfortable to watch it on their TV screens.

As the last hours ticked away, fears were expressed as to the damage to be caused by the largest non-nuclear, peacetime explosion in history. Campbell River feared the man-made earthquake would crack two nearby dams. A pulp mill, only six miles from the blast, was anxious about its 200-foot smokestack. If the engineers trying to alleviate these fears did not sound too convincing to some, that was because they were not at all sure themselves just what the blast would do!

The explosion would be triggered from a bunker, just 700 yards away, on Quadra Island. By dawn, April 5, all technicians were at their posts, although the weather caused anxiety. The leaden sky dimmed hopes. Favoring them, however, were southerly winds and high cloud level. These conditions were essential to clear away resulting gases.

While the clock entered its final circuit, the observation bunkers filled with more than 200 guests, mostly newsmen and photographers. On hand were Lieutenant-Governor Mr. Frank M. Ross, the federal minister of public works and his deputy, and the top officers of Western Canada's armed forces.

Zero hour was 9:31 a.m., carefully timed so northern tides would carry debris and gases into isolated waters. Sixteen minutes before the blast, the sky had so darkened as to indicate postponement. Then the first rocket was fired—the order was "Go."

"...Three...two...one...zero!" came the countdown, which had been delayed two minutes by an aircraft entering the danger-zone. A moment passed quietly as 5.3 miles of fuse flashed at the rate of 21,000 feet per second. Suddenly the green water became a surging white as a great bubble rushed to the surface. Sky vanished behind a flower-shaped smudge of rock and water that soared higher and higher, reaching an awesome 1,000 feet.

A monstrous, living thing—350,000 tons of rock fragments, 370,000 tons of water—the artichoke broadened, streaking toward the island shores at two miles per minute. The 2,750,000 pounds of Nitramex, detonating in split-second chain reaction, continued for long seconds; an eternity to the speechless observers.

Shock waves pummelled the bunkers, but without effect. Tidal waves slammed into rocky shores; again, without damage.

As the blast gradually subsided, the spectators' main anxiety was the result of 30 months' work and $3,000,000. Was Ripple Rock impotent at last?

To find out, RCMP *Victoria*, Lieutenant-Governor Ross and guests aboard, slowly approached the Narrows. From the south came RCMP *Nanaimo*. The patrol vessels neared, then passed each other... It is ironic that the first ship to steam over Ripple Rock was named after Victoria, the city which had had so much to say in its defence.

The enormous surgery was a complete success—at least 40 feet had been amputated from Old Rip's twin peaks.

The feared damage from the blast's shock waves never materialized, one of the greatest undertakings in Canadian history had been finished to perfection.

After 83 years of shipwreck and death, Ripple Rock's fangs had been pulled.

Chapter 11

Cape Cook Shipwrecks

A month-long race against death—"a tale of shipwreck, hardship and privation...of suffering and endurance almost beyond credence"—intrigued British Columbians, some 80 years ago.

This was the remarkable saga of the ill-fated Hawaiian barque *Thos. R. Foster*, which perished in the lethal grip of Vancouver Island's northwest coast, and of her heroic seamen who lived to tell the story.

"An unknown barque wrecked on the west coast—Indians bring the news—out of a crew of 20, 12 are drowned," cried the headlines, February 24, 1887.

Details of the tragedy were scant, little being known beyond the fact Indians had brought news of a ship lost with two-thirds of her crew near Clayoquot Sound, and that permission had been requested of Ottawa to dispatch the lighthouse tender *Sir James Douglas* to the rescue.

A week later, the *Douglas* returned to Victoria with Captain W.F. Rugg, his 17-man crew, and an exciting account of human stamina.

"We left Esquimalt on the evening of the 9th December for Honolulu with 1,650 tons of Wellington coal as cargo," Captain Rugg told a reporter. "We got outside the cape, all right, at daylight. On the afternoon of the 10th, took a S.W. gale and (the) ship commenced to make an unusual quantity of water on the 12th, and with constant laboring increased making water up till the 14th, when (I) found it necessary to call all hands to the pumps."

During the next 24 hours, the *Foster's* seamen had manned her pumps steadily. But it was a losing battle. With each passing hour, the seas lapped higher in her coal-laden holds, as a second sou'-wester bludgeoned her from above. Settling deeper in the raging sea, the

61

collier answered her helm sluggishly, forcing Rugg to abandon all attempts to maintain course, and, instead, limp before the wind for Cape Flattery's Neah Bay.

Early on the 16th, the weary master sighted a smudge on the horizon: Cape Flattery was 20 miles distant. But during the morning the gale subsided to "dead calm," only to veer around from the northeast and renew its assault on the beleaguered barque.

"I then headed (the) ship to the northward, trying to fetch the Vancouver Island shore, having six feet of water in the hold," Rugg recounted. "On the 17th, finding the ship laboring so heavily and water increasing, (I) had to keep (her) away for fear of staving her decks in, luffing her up when I saw a chance to do so.

"On the 18th, the haze over the land lit up and we sighted breakers under lead and head, which proved to be about eight miles to the east of Cape Cook. I then headed the ship to where I thought the smoothest place to ground her, (and) in order to save life, ran the ship in between the rocks as close as I could get until she took ground."

If it sounds easy — it wasn't.

For those aboard the doomed *Foster* had beached her in the worst stretch of jagged reefs and vicious storms to be found the length of Vancouver Island's west coast — worse even, than the dreaded Graveyard of the Pacific, known for a wreck for each mile.

Situated halfway between Kyuquot and Quatsino Sounds, Cape Cook — "a bold promontory," Captain Cook described it in 1778 — forms the craggy toe of Brooks Peninsula, a 60-square-mile boot of 2,500-foot hills and dense forests. A mile offshore rears barren Solander Island, inhabited only by sea lions, birds and stunted trees.

George Nicholson describes the region graphically: "Without a doubt, this 60-mile stretch of coastline, with its deep indentations, accounting for an additional several hundred miles, is the most desolate and God-forgotten piece of real estate in British Columbia...

"Viewed from the deck of a passing steamer, the scene today is the same as when Cook first saw it through his telescope. Not a wisp of smoke, not a tree disturbed, and the only sign of life, the sea birds and sea lions on Solander Island. Here one is about as far from civilization on Vancouver Island as it is possible to get."

This is the grim no-man's-land of reef and storm into which Captain Rugg skilfully urged his sinking command, over 80 years ago.

The leaking *Foster* had shuddered to a halt some distance from shore, her holds flooded to a depth of 13 feet. On deck, her frightened company fought to launch two of her lifeboats in the crashing surf, only to see them smashed to pieces against her side.

Desperately, the seamen launched their last hope, a smaller craft, against a rising crescendo of collapsing bulwarks and upperworks. The barque's canvas had long been ripped away, her compass and binnacle carried off in the surf.

Somehow, the first refugees reached the temporary safety of shore in their cockleshell boat, then completed two further trips between ship and shore with the remainder of their shipmates. Then, in the dark and cold, Captain Rugg took stock of the meagre supplies saved from the wreck. His check brought the full horror of their position home with hammer-like suddenness:

Eighteen men had to exist indefinitely on one box of soda crackers, a ham, "some bacon," and 30 cans of meat and fruit.

"In conversation with members of the crew," according to one account, "their life on the barren rocky shore was learned, and is a tale of hardship, suffering and endurance almost beyond credence. When they landed the first night all hands were played out by constantly being at the pumps for four days and nights without sleep.

"A small fire was lit and was the only seeming comfort they had during a freezing cold rainy night, lying on the rocks, some barefooted and in their shirt sleeves."

Several had been stripped naked while struggling through the surf, the surging waves even stealing shoes and socks, and were forced to obtain what pitiable warmth they could from the fire. In following days, some shoes, clothing and sail canvas washed ashore from the disintegrating barque, to be eagerly dried by those in need, the latter being used to fashion a crude tent.

Captain Rugg had maintained strict discipline from the first, rationing his men to a single cracker and a tiny bowl of brackish mussel and clam soup daily. With salvaged yarn, the shipwrecked mariners constructed snares; "when a seagull was caught it furnished a choice supper."

On the second day, Rugg ordered four men to start along the beach. The disheartened explorers returned the following day to report that way impossible. "Often they had to crawl over where a surefooted goat could scarcely pass, sometimes on their hands and knees through thick brush, often wading icy cold waters up to the shoulders, at all times suffering severely from lack of food and clothing."

After resting overnight, the seamen started again, on December 21, in the opposite direction. Three days from camp, on Christmas Eve, they decided a raft would afford faster travel and set about constructing the float of driftwood. Climbing aboard, they paddled awkwardly toward deep water, but, a quarter-mile from the beach, the raft suddenly broke apart, plunging them into the frigid sea.

Fortunately, all four reached a rocky islet where, after resting, they launched a large log into the surf. Straddling their ungainly, rolling command, the seamen paddled back to shore with sticks. Undaunted, they pressed onward, until finally barred by a river. Weak from hunger and exposure, without tools, they could do nothing but head back.

Eating the last of the precious rations Captain Rugg had jealously allotted them, some raw bacon, they turned toward camp. At a deserted fishing village, they stopped for the night, when one noticed four mice attacking the rotting head of a cod on the beach. Ever so carefully—it is not recorded how—the starving sailors captured the rodents, "which were boiled and considered a great delicacy."

Reaching camp at last, the men collapsed in exhaustion. Their fruitless trek had lasted eight days.

Rugg then detailed a party of 10 to try once more. This time their determination paid off. Three days out, they built a raft and successfully crossed an inlet to an island, the voyage by paddles of driftwood taking a full day. But their suffering was almost over, for, a day later, they sighted two Indian canoes.

Their hoarse shouts of joy soon brought the natives alongside, who rushed them to their camps near Kyuquot Sound, then rescued Captain Rugg and the others still on the beach. The fishermen could offer only boiled flour and dried salmon, "but these were luxuries" to the celebrating castaways.

Particularly after their attempts, towards the end, to cook kelp. The experiment had proven a failure, however, the kelp being "unpalatable."

The Indians nursed them as best they could for nine days, when they brought Father Nicolaye from Kyuquot, "who proved an angel of mercy to the shipwrecked seamen." The good priest soon had them transferred to his parish, boarding them in the village schoolhouse until word was sent to Victoria and the *Sir James Douglas* arrived 42 days later.

Brooding Cape Cook has known shipwreck too often over the years, even in the present day of miracle-working navigational aids. Eleven years before the ordeal of the *Thos. R. Foster*, another Hawaiian barque, the lumber-laden *Mauna Kea*, had crashed ashore after being adrift for two weeks. Unlike the *Foster*, three of *Mauna Kea's* men were lost.

When the rest of her crew did reach shore, it was to be seized by Indians who held them for ransom. HMS *Sparrowhawk* brought them to Victoria, unharmed, after two seamen escaped to Fort Rupert and sent word of their comrades' plight.

Mr. Nicholson records other vessels which have died near Cape Cook: the whaling schooner *Jane Gray* in May, 1893, a disaster which claimed 36 lives; the barque *William Foster*, 1901; sealing schooner *Triumph*, 1903, with all hands, and many more, mostly fishing vessels.

One of the more dramatic tragedies enacted in this haunted wilderness, and not unlike that of the *Thos. R. Foster*, was that of the Peruvian *Libertad*. Thirty-years-old, and loaded with Chilean nitrates for the Victoria Chemical Works, the 400-ton barque had been at sea a month, when "the vessel sprang a leak, having previously experienced terrible weather," wrote the *Colonist*. "The crew of 10 men were set to work at the pumps and the vessel continued northward, Captain Arena expecting to complete his voyage. He had not counted, however, on the weather experienced off the Pacific coast at this time of year, and as the barque continued to be driven northward the water continued to gain."

Steadily, *Libertad* had been battered northward, passing Cape Flattery and Juan de Fuca Strait. "The experience of the men must have been terrible, but in the way of South American mariners, when asked they simply hold up their hands and look piteously at the questioner."

For two bitter *months*, the Peruvians worked their pumps as the hungry seas reached ever higher, ever so slowly. Amazingly, during their incredible ordeal, they did not sight another vessel. They were alone, drifting steadily farther from land, on a sinking ship.

Finally, Captain Arena gave the order to abandon ship. "The largest boat on the barque was dropped from the davits, a sack full of bread was thrown into her and the crew got in, prepared to face almost anything in preference to further work at the pumps."

Captain Arena knew only that they were 50-60 miles from the northern end of Vancouver Island, "but of what they had to put up with after reaching shore, he knew nothing."

Despite a running sea, the Peruvians reached Cape Cook, safely landing amid the breakers in a small bay. Once ashore, the stranded seamen faced the same agonizing terror those of the *Foster* had endured years before: death by starvation or exposure, miles from rescue.

For four torturous days, they trudged, crawled, climbed and waded southward, eating mussels when the tide was out, starving when it was in. "Oh, how hungry," said one in broken English, upon rescue. "Sometimes we crawled like cats; other times climbed like monkeys, but all the time walk and no food."

Four days and four nights later, they stumbled into the camp of three prospectors, to learn that in their desperate trek to safety, they had achieved but four miles. The sailors' ordeal had not ended entirely, however, the heroic miners risking their own lives and limbs in leading them to civilization.

Today Cape Cook is as lonely as ever, visited only by the occasional trapper and Indian fisherman, and the sea lion, unchanged since the perilous days of sail when ships and men fought and died in her desolate arena.

Chapter 12

Shipwreck, Ordeal and Death on Victoria's Doorstep

A savage winter gale rattled Victoria windows in the early hours of February 24, 1862. But aside from spiriting away a few hats, the sou'-wester caused only mild discomfort. By late morning "old friend Boreas" had been forgotten, his brief visit marked only by a tongue-in-cheek paragraph in the *Colonist*.

Victorians eagerly turned to lengthy, exciting accounts of the raging American Civil War. But it was "friend" Boreas who again claimed the headlines February 27. For it had just been learned that, although the city had escaped without injury his attention two nights before, the schooner *Tolo* had not been as lucky.

"We have sad news to lay before our readers this morning," said the newspaper. "The sloop *Rambler*, Captain Frank, arrived last night from Port Townsend, having on board Francis J. Bryne, mate, and Peter Nelson and John Sullivan, two of the crew of the schooner *Tolo*, which vessel they report was capsized opposite the American station on San Juan Island, on Monday morning last, and Captain Maloney, four passengers and one seaman drowned."

Although reports of disaster at sea were only too familiar to a busy port like Victoria, residents thrilled to the exciting report of shipwreck, ordeal and death which had occurred almost on their doorstep while they slept safe in warm beds...

The Port Ludlow schooner was almost new. She had cleared Victoria February 23, bound for her homeport with 25 tons of freight. Without ballast, she ran high and light before the raging gale. On deck, her weary master, 36-year-old Captain Maloney, had been on watch for hours. *Tolo* was not handling well, the lack of ballast and her tall, heavy spars threatening to heel her over at any moment.

66

Finally came a slight lull in the storming darkness, and, relinquishing command to First Mate Francis Bryne, Maloney retired to his cabin for some needed rest.

He had just turned in when disaster struck. It was 6 a.m. Without warning, the southerly wind veered from the southwest. A sudden gust from the unexpected quarter flipped little *Tolo* onto her beam. In seconds, she had filled until only her deep keel remained above the surface.

Now 12 persons were struggling frantically for their lives.

For two passengers, asleep in their berths, the struggle was pathetically—or mercifully—brief. San Francisco theatrical agent R.A. Eddy and a young farmer, John Cox, were trapped in their submerged cabin; neither was seen again.

Now there were 10.

Nine, including Captain Maloney, had been flung into the threshing sea.

Peter Nelson was at the helm when *Tolo* capsized. As he felt the schooner going, he jumped to the rail and clambered over her turning side. Seconds later, he was clinging to the keel and fighting to haul Mate Bryne to the slippery perch. *Tolo's* upended weight kept her relatively steady in the heaving seas, much like modern oil-drilling rig, but her exposed keel was awash.

Pounded by each wave, Nelson dragged Bryne to his precarious sanctuary. Still gasping for breath, mouth, eyes and nostrils smarting from salt spray, the two then "turned their attention to the others, who were struggling in the water or clinging to the side of the schooner."

Sadly, there was little they could do for their drowning comrades...

Nearest was seaman John Sullivan. Fingers already numbed by the intense cold, Nelson and Bryne knotted their heavy jackets together. Gripping a sleeve, they cast the other to Sullivan, who secured the coarse, reluctant material about his waist. Then, ever so carefully, they drew him to the keel. He, too, was safe—for the moment.

In the precious minutes it had taken to haul Sullivan aboard, the sea had been claiming the others. With heartrending cries and "despairing looks," Second Mate William Sherlock, the Anderssen brothers, seamen, the Chinese cook, and a passenger named Ehlers had been floundering alongside the wreck. Some desperately gripped pieces of rigging. Waves battered numb fingers, breaking their hold...For these unfortunates, the end came in a matter of minutes.

Some were overcome by the cold and sank quickly. Others tried to scale *Tolo's* slippery, round bottom to the sanctuary of the keel. Hands cut and bleeding, they would grab at the outstretched arms of Sullivan, Nelson and Byrne, but to no avail. One by one they were swept away.

Now there were five.

William Carter seemed to have a better chance. The portly, mustachioed passenger from Portsmouth, Maine, managed to grasp a fender and skylight which had been launched when *Tolo* overturned. Holding one under each arm, middle-aged Carter cut a pathetically comical figure as he drifted away on towering waves. Above the wind's roar, he yelled, "I'm going to try to make the shore!"

His work was cut out for him—San Juan Island was five miles distant.

All this time—actually only minutes, although it must have seemed an eternity—poor Captain Maloney had been clinging to the main chains. Being an excellent swimmer did not help. Half-dressed, half-submerged, the unbearable cold was fast draining his strength. Now began the saddest chapter of the *Tolo* tragedy.

Nelson, Bryne and Sullivan still rode *Tolo's* keel. Encouraging Maloney to hold on just a bit longer, they wrestled with their clothing to make a lifeline. Actually, it may have been Maloney who gave encouragement. Courageous to the end, he coolly gave his men instructions as to how to save him. But stiff fingers refused to co-ordinate; irretrievable seconds were lost before they finally had the makeshift line ready.

Casting a sleeve to Maloney, they slowly reeled in the slack. Eagerly, he clutched the sleeve, felt himself being dragged upward to safety. Because *Tolo* was almost new, having completed only three voyages, there was little marine growth on her bottom—nothing for Maloney to grab.

When one of the crude knots suddenly pulled free there was nothing he could do to stop his fall; he was back where he had started, clutching the chains, just head and shoulders above water.

Now the weakening trio on the keel painfully knotted a neck-comforter to an oil slicker. Maloney tied the sleeve around his neck, gripping the cuff between chattering teeth. This time no knot slipped. Said the *Colonist:* "The coat was made of inferior material, and at the first pull the sleeve was torn out and poor Maloney exclaimed that he was afraid he could not be saved, as he was growing weak and benumbed.

"Several other ineffectual attempts to save their captain were made, and at last the survivors, finding further exertion useless, reluctantly abandoned him to his fate..."

It was a painful decision, but unavoidable. Exhausted by their futile attempts at rescue, blue from the excruciating cold, the three men watched the final, sad act of Maloney's personal tragedy. When the poor skipper realized they could do no more for him, his submerged legs now paralyzed, he cried, "Boys, don't forget my wife and children —oh, my poor wife!"

He repeated this several times. Then, almost imperceptibly, he squared his shoulders, thrust out his jaw and released his hold on the chains. To have been so close to safety..! Arms outspread, only his head above water, Maloney slowly drifted astern, occasionally raising his eyes to "gaze wistfully and sadly towards the floating wreck above him, and at the men clinging to it, then his head would slowly droop again.

"When he had floated about half a length astern, he raised his head, as with a last effort...called out feebly, 'Boys, don't forget my poor wife and children'—and tossed his arms above his head, and with a gurgling cry, sank beneath the waves."

Haunted by Maloney's entreaties, the survivors now remembered passenger Carter. For 10 minutes they watched him riding the waves with fender and skylight still tucked under each arm. Finally, he vanished in the distance, never to be seen again.

Now there were three.

The derelict drifted with wind and tide, its three reluctant passengers "exposed to the pitiless pelting of the snowstorms which have prevailed for several days past, without a morsel of food, suffering greatly, the seas occasionally making a clean breach over them."

Hours passed. Frostbitten, frightened and hungry, Bryne, Nelson and Sullivan anxiously scanned the ragged horizon for sign of a ship. Nothing. Soon they had become so stiff they could not even turn their heads to look for the help that was not coming. It became so cold their soaked clothing froze on their bodies. Noon came and passed. Then it was evening again, and the temperature dropped further.

Victoria reported a foot of snow overnight.

That night was the longest of their lives. Even the welcome appearance of a pallid morning sun failed to cheer them. They were losing hope. But their ordeal was far from ended. Another noon, another night. Now it was February 26. They had been adrift for 48 hours. Still no ship came. Hands and feet were so numb they could no longer hold onto the keel, the men simply draping themselves over it. Periodically, a larger wave would almost sweep them away, knocking them about like pieces of driftwood against a shore.

A third noon came and went.

At 2 p.m. that afternoon—56 hours after *Tolo* capsized—the sloop *Random* chanced upon the wreck, now off Lopez Island. Enroute to Victoria from Port Townsend, an amazed Captain Frank answered their feeble, rasping cries for help. Strangely, he heard, rather than saw them. *Random* had made it just in time, the exhausted survivors admitting that another few hours would have meant the end.

That evening, they were in Victoria, wards of an incredulous city. Everyone marvelled that such an adventure had occurred so near home. With fresh clothing, warm food and "proper medical treatment, no fears are entertained but that all three will soon fully recover from the effects of the exposure."

It was then learned that one of the victims, a Canadian known only as Ehler, would not have been aboard *Tolo* but for the generosity of Captain Maloney. Ehler had come to Victoria from San Francisco to meet a friend who was to get him a job. But, upon arrival, he could not find his friend and good-natured Maloney had grubstaked the man and granted him free passage to Port Ludlow to work in a lumber mill.

The public gladly donated $210 to the three survivors, who "suitably remunerated" their savior, Captain Frank.

By now *Tolo* had drifted almost into San Juan Harbor. Two men "camped" aboard her hull for a night to claim salvage, but the next tide carried her away again. Off Lopez Island once more, salvors swarmed aboard the derelict with cable to anchor her. One of the salvage ships, the schooner *Mink,* had good reason to remember the gale which claimed *Tolo;* she had lost every stitch of sail in the blow.

Fifteen longboat crews then hooked the hull in an unsuccessful bid to muscle her into harbor. When former mate Francis Bryne arrived to take charge of the wreck for her owners, the salvors hustled him back aboard the *Random* with blunt instructions as to just what he could tell his employers! But Bryne returned with reinforcements, a squad of soldiers from the American garrison. The salvors now recognized his claim and departed — at bayonet-point.

Days later, *Tolo* had been righted and towed into Port Townsend for repairs.

Meanwhile, one of the survivors had not been recovering as expected. Poor John Sullivan was taken to Townsend Marine Hospital where it was feared he would lose both feet to frostbite.

Two days after the *Tolo* tragedy, San Juan had claimed another victim. This time it was not the island, but San Juan Harbor, on Vancouver Island's west coast. The New Granadian bark *Anna Barnard,* fron San Francisco for piles and lumber at Sooke, had driven ashore in thick weather. The old sailer broke in two within minutes. Captain Olmstead and two volunteers, the cook and a seaman, lowered a boat and tried to make shore for help. When the tiny craft splintered against the rocks, Olmstead's heroic companions were drowned.

Fortunately, the master reached land, while the remainder of his crew, seven men, perched in the wreck's rigging for six hours, when low tide permitted them to walk ashore. Nearby Indians cared for the shipwrecked mariners, then canoed them to Victoria.

It had been a bad month for those who went down to the sea in ships. Besides *Tolo* and the *Barnard,* there had been several other mishaps: A man identified only as "Alick" drowned while trying to

70

recover his sloop which had drifted away and subsequently wrecked. Venerable *Princess Royal* grounded while clearing Victoria, but was refloated by the steamer, *Otter*. The sloop *Black Hawk* went down in another gale off San Juan Island, with two men and a woman.

Finally, a dismasted bark was sighted off Neah Bay, Wash. The *Colonist,* however, believed its informant had mistaken his position and sighted the wreckage of old *Anna Barnard*.

Chapter 13

Agony of the Valencia

In terms of lives lost, there have been greater marine disasters than that of the 1,600-ton, 24-year-old American steamship *Valencia,* 70 years ago. However, in terms of human tragedy—of sheer, unadulterated horror—there can have been few wrecks of equal magnitude.

"It was in the blackness of a winter night, lashed by a howling gale and blinded by freezing sleet, that the fine steamer *Valencia* crashed onto the jagged rocks of the west coast of Vancouver Island near Cape Beale. It was 15 minutes before midnight, on January 22, 1906. In the next 48 hours 117 persons perished miserably in one of the worst marine horrors known to that strip of coast....

"There were other shipping disasters when even more lives were lost, but never had such a catastrophe occurred under such circumstances; when rescue vessels standing off, impotent to give aid, as pounding waves hammered the doomed ship to pieces and snatched and clawed helpless men and women from the rigging to destruction; and high above the crumbling and shapeless *Valencia,* men watched helplessly as passengers and crewmen died before their eyes...."

So wrote the late Bruce McKelvie, dean of British Columbia historians, of the wreck of the Ss *Valencia.*

Bound for Seattle, *Valencia* had cleared San Francisco on January 20, in fair weather, to encounter dense fog off Cape Mendocino. With lookouts posted forward, whistle blowing, the steamer inched northward. Seven hours before she struck the rocks, three miles east of Pachena Point on Vancouver Island's exposed west coast, Captain Johnston had ordered Boatswain Tim McCarthy to prepare two leads for sounding. With two other crewmen and the chief officer,

McCarthy had also used the Thompson sounding machine, detecting no bottom at 250 fathoms.

Hours later, carried 20 miles off course by powerful currents, *Valencia* hit the shore. At first the engines had remained functioning, McCarthy testified at the inquest, and Captain Johnston had ordered his crew of eight seamen and four quartermasters to lower all seven boats to the saloon rail. In almost complete darkness, McCarthy and fellow crewmen fought to lower the boats as they were crowded by passengers who milled anxiously about the rail.

Despite Johnston's order, the four forward boats were launched immediately, McCarthy recounting: "...Most of them were full of passengers and there was a strain on the tackles. Of these four boats, only one, No. 2, got away from the ship's side. There was a heavy sea running; was breaking almost to the bridge, and I am doubtful if those boats could have got away even in daylight. The captain turned the searchlight all around. I saw No. 2 boat off at some little distance; then someone pulled the whistle and the electric light went out.

"I saw No. 1 boat smash alongside. There would be 15 or 20 people in her. I had a ladder thrown over, also some ropes and I saw one man climb aboard."

When the dying ship heeled sharply to port, No. 7 lifeboat was launched, followed by No. 6 and one of the *Valencia's* three liferafts. The remainder of those aboard, almost a hundred souls, clutched the ship's rigging or huddled on the hurricane deck as officers sought to reassure them of rescue in the ghostly glare of rockets being fired by Captain Johnston.

By this time, reported McCarthy, only the social hall and the weather side of the saloon remained dry.

First to learn of the disaster was the lighthouse keeper at Cape Beale when a handful of survivors, among the first to leave the ship, staggered to his door. He immediately flashed word to Victoria by telegraph (one of the few occasions, fortunately, when the lines were not down when needed most). Immediately, the vessels *Queen* and *City of Topeka,* and the powerful tug *Salvor,* steamed northward to the rescue. Tragically, as in so many other West Coast marine disasters, high hopes, good intentions and raw courage were to prove futile against the might of the Pacific.

For when the rescue fleet reached the scene, they realized from the outset that nothing could be done for *Valencia's* dying company. Impaled on rocks at the base of sheer sliffs, swept by each incoming wave, the steamer had already buckled under the onslaught. Despite this, *Salvor* made a brave attempt to rescue her, and succeeded in approaching to within a half-mile of the wreck when her master was forced to retreat. *Salvor's* mighty engines simply could not defy the vacuum-like tide and breakers which threatened, at every moment, to pull her onto the rocks with the *Valencia.*

Aboard the steamer, Second Officer P.E. Petterson and 40 others, clinging to the splintered vessel's rigging, had watched *Salvor's* valiant bid to reach them, hearts breaking when they saw her put about. One of *Valencia's* 37 survivors, he later described to the coroner's jury how they had despaired at the tug's retreat.

Years after, former officer of the *Salvor,* Captain Ernest Jordan, recalled that agonizing rescue attempt for Mr. McKelvie, stating: "When it was found that the vessel could not approach close enough to shoot a line aboard the wreck, I offered to try and get closer in a lifeboat to, if possible, float a line down to the *Valencia.* I was not permitted to make the attempt, which even at the time I realized offered but a hundred-to-one chance of success."

Thus *Salvor* had retreated, to wait, with the equally frustrated *Queen* and *Topeka,* for the inevitable. "It was terrible to stand off there and watch the wreck break up, and see the people who were in the rigging drop off into the boiling sea," said Jordan.

Aboard the *Valencia,* Bosun McCarthy's bid for safety came the next morning when, upon seeing that several of those who had left the ship earlier had reached shore, Captain Johnston asked him if he would take the remaining boat, No. 5, to the beach with a lifeline.

Minutes later, McCarthy and a frightened crew cast off, having been lowered by Captain Johnston (who, all survivors agreed, carried out his duties heroically to the very end) himself. As those aboard the *Valencia* cheered, they vanished in the mist, having "got away with considerable difficulty."

"We kept outside the breakers but at times could not see the shore; it was so thick and we could not find a place to land.

"I came to some rocks which I took to be the Durkin Rocks off Tatooche (Tatoosh Island, Cape Flattery), and finally a heavy sea hit us and two of the men lost their oars and we had only two left (having broken one in leaving the ship). We pulled a little farther and one of the men said he thought it was the Vancouver Island shore. Finally we made a landing in a place I afterwards found to be between Pachena Bay and Cape Beale."

Then they had begun a two-hour, exhausting hike along the rugged shore to Cape Beale, lightkeeper Thomas Paterson alerting Victoria by telegraph, as three Clo-oose settlers hiked overland to the scene with ropes and supplies in an attempt to rescue *Valencia's* company by land. Sadly, by the time they reached the cliffs towering above the ship, only 60-odd persons remained in her rigging and on her flooded poop deck.

(Earlier, Second Mate Pettersen and six others had escaped on a raft, several men and all of the women having refused to leave the ship after witnessing what had happened to so many others. When the

74

Topeka picked them up, Pettersen and comrades were the last to escape from the *Valencia,* another raft having made its break previously, and eventually drifting ashore).

When the overland party reached the cliffs, they found a lifeline snagged in the rocks. However, upon reeling it in, the thin hawser snapped—even as the unfortunates below cheered at their apparent salvation. Then, like those aboard the ships standing out to sea, the trio had witnessed the final act of the tragedy. For, unable to reach the ship from shore, Captain Johnston having long since used his last rocket to fire a line ashore, when there had been no one there to secure it, they could only join in the death watch.

Finally—40 horrendous hours after the *Valencia* struck—it was over, the last of her doomed company plucked from her collapsed rigging. The most infamous shipwreck in provincial history was ended.

A grim footnote to this tragedy was added in 1933, when old No. 5 lifeboat was found drifting in Barkley Sound. Where it had been for 27 years, we can but marvel. Adding to the eeriness of the discovery was the fact that her paint was still good after more than a quarter-century's exposure to the elements. Or would this indicate that the ghostly craft had been sheltered, perhaps in one of the many sea caves to be found along Vancouver Island's west coast? More than once it had been rumored that lifeboats, manned by skeletons, had been sighted by fishermen.

Five months after the disaster, Indian fisherman Clanewah Tom and his wife, scouring the adjacent beaches in their canoe, were attracted by the gaping mouth of a sea cave. Intrigued by the sandstone cleft, Tom swam inside, only to beat a hasty retreat. Rushing to authorities, he claimed to have seen a lifeboat inside the cave, afloat and manned by eight skeletons.

Upon hearing Clanewah Tom's breathless account, Carmanah lightkeeper W.P. Daykin dispatched his two sons to investigate. Even the lighthouse tender *Quadra* made an attempt at locating the mystery lifeboat. But Tom's discovery of the sea cave must have occurred at a freak turn of tide, for the searchers could not enter due to the relentless surf. And the mystery of the skeleton-manned lifeboat remains unsolved.

A yellowing account from an old Vancouver *Province* noted: "Discussion arose as to whether this boat was one of the *Valencia's* or whether it solved the mystery of the missing men of the *King David*. When this British ship was wrecked at Bajo Point, Notka Sound, in the previous December, a boat's crew left for Cape Beale to seek help. The rest of the crew stayed on the rocks and after 33 days there marooned, were taken off by a passing vessel. The boat's crew was never seen or heard of again."

Surprisingly, the *Valencia* horror has occurred not once but several times—if one believes reports which have circulated among the West Coast marine fraternity for 70 years.

In 1910 the Seattle *Times* reported a spectre which had been observed in Vancouver Island's Graveyard of the Pacific: "During the past summer, persistent rumors were brought into Seattle by sailors on vessels frequently in and out of the cape, of a phantom ship seen off the dangerous coast of Vancouver Island.

"They said it resembled the ill-fated *Valencia,* which went down in those waters a few, short years ago with more than 100 souls, and that they could vaguely see human forms clinging to her masts and rigging. On some occassions the spectacle seemed immobile, and again the mystery was accentuated by the fact that the phantom moved steadily with the ship of those who watched, maintaining its relative position perfectly. Again it leaped upon the rocks where the real ship met destruction..."

Hallucination, optical illusion, or—? Who knows.

Again, we can only ponder. If ever a ship could be haunted, it is ill-starred *Valencia* and her lost 117.

Chapter 14

Incredible Last Voyage of the Clara Nevada

GOLD! From the frozen wilderness of the Yukon came the magic word in 1897 which was to hold an eager world breathless for two exciting years. By liner, freighter, condemned hulk and homemade rowboat, thousands, from every corner of the globe, every walk of life, answered the siren call of untold riches.

Overland, from Skagway, Copper River, Ashcroft and Edmonton, it was by rail, stage, horse, oxen, dog, canoe, raft and foot. Distance, hardship and death deterred few.

The resulting demand for shipping — of any size, description and state of seaworthiness — created the greatest boom in Northwest history. Not since the trail of '58 had British Columbia, Washington and Oregon seen such a rag-tag fleet of "ships."

One of the motley hundreds hastily thrown into service was the three-masted steamer *Clara Nevada*. Like many another member of the gold fleet, she was to suffer the supreme penalty of avarice. In fact, when, today, considering her age, condition and crew, it is little less than amazing that she ever cleared her Seattle berth!

February 14, 1898, the crack steamer *Islander* sent word from Union Bay, B.C., that "the steamer *Clara Nevada,* which left Dyea and Skagway on Saturday afternoon, February 5, has so far failed to report to Juneau. As she was carrying several passengers from Skagway to Juneau her not reaching there looks badly.

"Some steamer has met with disaster near Seward City, 50 miles north of Juneau. Some parties claim to have seen a steamer on fire and heard an explosion, and passengers say that the *Clara Nevada* was on fire on the trip up and had to have her boilers repaired. The beach near Seward City is strewn with wreckage, some of it painted in the same coloring as the *Nevada*. The wreckage was seen by Captain Thomas Latham of the steamer *Coleman,* which arrived at Juneau from Skagway. The captain and crew all think it is the *Nevada*...

"There appears to be no question but that some boat has come to grief, and as the *Nevada* is the only boat not accounted for, it is thought to be her. All hands are supposed to be lost, about 40 people."

Built in 1872 as the *Hassler* for the U.S. Geodetic Survey, the ill-fated steamer had been condemned after 26 years' service. With the sudden inexhaustible demand for ships, the newly-founded Pacific & Alaskan Transportation Company purchased the aging steamer, renaming her *Clara Nevada* after a popular actress. Hastily outfitted to carry 200 passengers and 300 tons of freight, the *Nevada* entered upon her new career. It was to be deathly short.

Clara Nevada had cleared Seattle with 200 passengers and crew, touching at Port Townsend and Fort Simpson in British Columbia, before reaching Skagway. It was upon her return voyage that she met with disaster.

When the first reports of her loss reached Seattle, her drowned company was soon forgotten in a riot of accusation, name-calling and slander which was not to be forgotten — or forgiven — for many years after.

"COFFIN SHIP...An unsafe, ill-equipped craft with a drunken and blasphemous crew... A passenger tells of the many horrors of the *Clara Nevada's* trip northward... Terrible tale told by a man who for safety transferred to the *Islander*..." screamed the black headlines of the *Seattle Daily Times,* days later.

"The terrible story of the *CN's* wreck, with the loss of some 60 lives, grows worse as more light is thrown upon the vessel's condition when she left Seattle," thundered the *Times.* "One hundred and fifty passengers and an immense amount of valuable merchandise left this port in an unsafe vessel and in charge of a drunken and blasphemous crew over which a brave captain, a gentlemanly purser and a refined freight clerk sought to exercise the authority granted them by law. That she ever reached her destination is one of those modern miracles which God sometimes works in spite of man's failings, avarice, incompetence and greed.

"The whole story of that north-bound trip excels anything that has ever been told of a voyage on this Pacific Coast. It is a story that should bring the blush of shame upon the cheeks of the owners of that vessel, and that should bring the righteous indignation of an outraged public upon the heads of the culpable inspectors at this port."

The story behind this devastating broadside is as shocking today as it was to readers of 80 years ago.

According to several passengers of that memorable voyage to the goldfields, the entire trip had been a comedy of errors which escaped becoming tragedy only through, as the *Times* noted, a miracle.

"I was afraid that (she) would be wrecked from the time she left Seattle until Skagway was reached," stormed Charles Jones of The Dalles, Ore. "We smashed into the U.S. revenue cutter *Grant* when we were backing out from the Yesler dock; we rammed into almost every wharf at which we tried to land; we blew out three flues; we foundered around in rough water until all the passengers were scared almost to death. We witnessed intoxication among the officers, and heard them cursing each other until it was sickening. It was an awful trip, and I would not have gone aboard that boat again under any circumstances."

Just four hours out of Seattle, alarmed passengers had circulated a petition requesting custom officials at the next port-of-call, Port Townsend, detain the unlucky ship, that they might transfer to another, safer craft. A majority of those who had not fled to the blind sanctuary of their cabins signed the document, while Alaskan hotel-keeper M.R. King, R.C. Smelzer and another gentleman were appointed a committee to plead their case with customs. Alas, the officer replied "he did not have the authority to hold the boat, but took the names of the committee. When the petition was offered him he handed it back, saying that it would do no good, as he could not act."

"Not four hours out of port and found in such a condition! Is there any excuse under high heaven that the inspectors at this port can offer for this state of affairs aboard that boat?" raged the *Times*.

The *Nevada's* arrival at Port Townsend had further jarred frayed nerves when she rammed the wharf, "smashing our bowsprit, to say nothing of the damage done to the wharf. This made us still more anxious to hold the boat, but we were powerless and she got her papers."

Which leaves readers of today wondering which the frantic passengers prized more, their lives or the unused (and probably non-refundable) portions of their tickets?

Whatever, the terrified company remained with the ship, to experience misadventure after misadventure. Heavy seas near Fort Simpson strained the *Nevada's* ancient boilers, blowing out three flues. Twelve hours were spent at Simpson making repairs. Continuing on — somehow — to Skagway, the ill-starred vessel made port safely, if not happily, as passengers virtually scrambled down the gangplank to again reach *terra firma*.

"She was not in charge of proper persons," Jones opined. "Two-thirds of them were drunk.

"The second mate was put in penance 24 hours, commencing after we left Port Townsend. The first mate was full the night we left Seattle. He drank all the time, but was yet able to be around and issue orders. The steward was drunk all the time. I never heard such language as was used by the waiters, mates and stewards. They abused each other shamefully, and made it very disagreeable for the passengers."

As for the engineers, he had not "heard that (they) were drunk. (But) the freight clerk told me that the first engineer was taken on because he was a Mason, and not because he was a competent man. The freight clerk told me distinctly that as a matter of fact the engineer was incompetent.

"The captain, purser and freight clerk attended strictly to business and were gentlemen."

One of the petition committee, R.C. Smelzer, had originally planned returning upon the *Nevada* but, after the voyage north, changed his mind. When the hell ship cleared Skagway, with some 63 passengers, "five or six of whom were women," one of those watching her depart was Mr. Smelzer. As the old ship wheezed seaward, Smelzer recalled his last conversation with Captain C.H. Lewis.

The worried master "told me that if he ever got the *Nevada* back to Seattle in safety she would never go out with him again unless she was in proper shape. He said her hull was all right, but that she needed new machinery. The captain claimed that when the *Nevada* was being remodeled and fitted the owners would not listen to him, but did things to suit themselves.

"On one occasion Captain Lewis said that if he called on the engineer to back up he was sure to go ahead."

The scathing reports of Messrs. Jones and Smelzer, "corroborated by 14 others," aroused indignation and anger throughout the Northwest and Alaska. Among them was second steward Fred Emery, who reported a "hard trip up...the steamer acting like an old tub and the majority of the crew keeping drunk and fighting the greater part of the time, the rowdy element being so conspicious that the steward, Dan O'Donnell, would have been thrown overboard on the trip had not the captain interfered."

As the controversy spread, most newspapers echoing the bitter charges and counter charges, the steamship *Rustler* continued rescue operations. She had easily located the *Nevada's* grave, a reef off Eldred Rock, Lynn Canal; the death ship lay in four fathoms, only her spars and a lifeboat, entangled in the rigging, showing at low tide.

The *Rustler's* search had been aided by reports of George Beck and his wife, of Seward City, who had watched a small steamer "well out in the channel, at first bucking a head wind and afterwards breaking out in flames." Days later, nearby beaches were littered with wreckage, lifeboats and a fragment of the *Nevada's* nameboard, bearing three letters. Some debris was charred, while most showed no signs of fire. Heavy snow obscured all bodies, no survivors were found.

Inspection by divers of the submerged hull indicated the theory of

RCN salvage operations in Sydney Inlet, where another so-called mystery wreck challenged modern-day technology. How many vessels died, unsung, along the treacherous British Columbia coast was never known. [Inset] Naval personnel examine some of the intriguing artifacts which were recovered from one such unidentified wreck in Vancouver Island's Sydney Inlet.

When the old steamer Alpha wrecked off Denman Island, nearby beaches were strewn with wreckage. One settler salvaged two stools, a hatch cover, which he made into a checker board, some plush cushions [still in use in 1959], an 18-foot ladder and a hardwood panel.

After an active career as one of Her Majesty's gunboats, the steamer Grappler *assumed a new career as coastal freighter; only to meet death, sudden and violent, when fire erupted below decks.*

July 19, 1942, the Second World War came to the Pacific Coast when the Japanese submarine I-25 torpedoed and shelled the Victoria-built freighter Fort Camosun. *Kept afloat only by her cargo of plywood the stricken steamer is shown here while under tow, with the corvette HMS Edmunston alongside. The Camosun's torpedoing off Cape Flattery was the first of only two such incidents on this coast throughout the Second World War.*

1

2

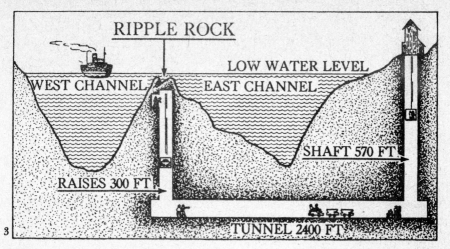

RIPPLE ROCK

LOW WATER LEVEL

WEST CHANNEL — EAST CHANNEL

SHAFT 570 FT

RAISES 300 FT

TUNNEL 2400 FT

3

(1) *9:31 a.m. April 5, 1958—zero hour. After years of posing as a deadly threat to shipping, Ripple Rock's fangs were pulled by almost 1,400 pounds of high explosive. The largest peacetime explosion in history, and a major Canadian engineering feat.*
(2) *A mushroom-like cloud shortly after the blast.*
(3) *A sketch showing the tunnels and shafts they were dug in order to get under and into the Rock for placing the explosive charge.*
(4) *Navigation chart of Seymour Narrows at Ripple Rock.*
(5) *Ready for a bird's-eye view of the greatest non-nuclear explosion in history: the observation bunkers overlooking Ripple Rock.*

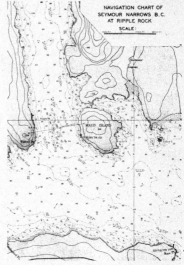

NAVIGATION CHART OF
SEYMOUR NARROWS B.C.
AT RIPPLE ROCK
SCALE

4

5

Although not the worst shipwreck in British Columbia history in terms of the number of lives lost, the American steamship Valencia has gone down in the record books as being the worst shipwreck in terms of terror: "Never had such a catastrophe occured under such circumstances..."

(Center) In happier days, passengers clamber aboard the Valencia en route to Nome. (Below, left) Only a few of her company survived, shown here battling their way to the rescue ship City of Topeka. Others pose for pictures aboard the rescue vessel.

Ss. Pacific. *Built 25 years before colliding with the* Orpheus *to "supply a sudden demand for shipping in the California trade," the sidewheeler had not been considered a safe vessel 17 years before her last voyage... (Inset) Capt. Jefferson D. Howell, her master, had had an exciting career. Brother-in-law of Confederate President Jefferson Davis, and hero of the rebel navy, he had skippered several coastal steamers.*

In Seattle, the sinking of the ill-starred Clara Nevada *sparked a war of words which is remembered to this day.*

More than once, the Canadian Pacific coastal steamer Princess Maquinna and her crew were called upon to defy the elements to aid seamen in distress. Before sighting the stranded sailing vessel Carelmapu, in November of 1915, the Maquinna's Captain Edward Gillam had had a premonition of impending disaster. The violent storm which delivered the Chilean windjammer's death blow also did its best to wreck the Maquinna. (Below) The Carelmapu near Gowland Rocks off Portland Point with distress flags flying.

(Top) *The* Hazelton *coming out of Kitselas Canyon, Skeena River, B.C.* (Below) *High in the* Mount Royal's *wheelhouse, Captain Johnson felt his ship shudder as she nudged the island, even before he could think. Then the* Mount Royal *groaned to a stop, her spoon-like bow impaled on the rocks.*

Victoria's Fisherman's Wharf. Here, minutes after clearing her Inner Harbor berth, the steamer Cariboo's *boiler exploded, killing the last of the Jamieson brothers. (Inset) Francis Barnard. He survived the wreck of the* Fort Yale, *which claimed the life of Smith Jamieson. Barnard went on to found the famous B.X. Stage line.*

The dying barque Coloma *off Cape Beale... In recent years divers searching for the ill-famed* Tonquin, *victim of Indian attack and explosion, discovered the remains of this American sailing vessel which brought undying fame for Minnie Paterson, "Grace Darling of the Pacific Northwest."*

The rock and island-strewn waters near Cape Beale.

Alerted by Captain Christensen that the company of the barque John Bright *had been massacred by Hesquiat Indians, HMS* Sparrowhawk *sailed northward to investigate. Sadly, due to Governor Seymour's reluctance to believe Christen's initial reports, she was too late.*

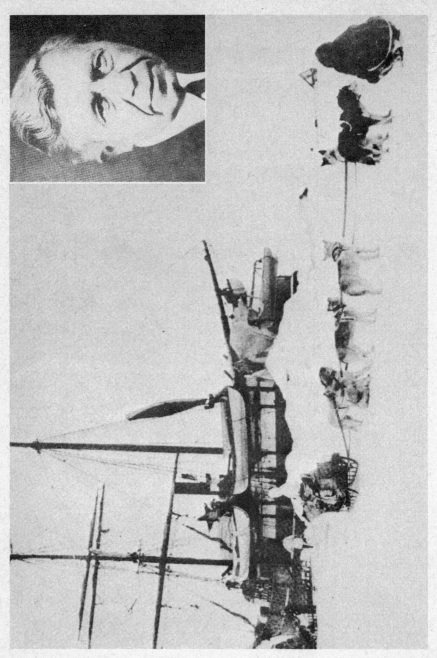

The old steamer Karluk, caught in the ice off Cross Island. Here, Vilhjalmur Stefannson and three companions prepare to hunt for caribou. They were never to see the Canadian Arctic Expedition's flagship again. (Inset) Manitoba-born Arctic explorer and scientist Vilhjalmur Stefansson, whose work inspired the tragic Canadian Arctic Expedition of 1913 which sailed from Victoria to the rousing strains of military bands and cheering crowds—and ended in shipwreck in the frozen Arctic wastes.

The Clara Nevada, *originally called the* Hassler, *a United States Government survey ship, had been condemned and sold. She was given new life during the Klondike gold rush, carrying freight and passengers to Skagway and Dyea. In 1908, after another vicious gale swept Lynn Canal, her bones were surrendered from the sea and deposited on shore.*

The CPR steamer Tees.

1

2

(1) *The sleek passenger liner* Princess Sophia *at Juneau, Alaska.*
(2) *This an an actual photograph of the* Princess Sophia *foundering on Vanderbilt Reef in the Lynn Canal on October 24, 1918. All aboard perished. This photo is taken from the windward side just hours before the big ship was swept over the reef and sank.*
(3) *The* Princess Sophia *during World War I.*

Victoria's beautiful Ross Bay Cemetery. More than one shipwrecked mariner found a final resting place in this tranquil setting beside Juan de Fuca Strait.

her destruction by the explosion of her boilers was correct, "the vessel being torn and twisted amidships so that her floating life after the explosion must have been limited to seconds, while the weather was too rough for the boats to avail anyone."

Inspiring salvage attempts were rumors that one party of passengers had been heading "outside" with up to $120,000.

When the steamer *Thistle* docked at Victoria from Skagway, her officers reported "Feeling runs high at the Lynn Canal ports again against the inspectors who permitted the *Nevada* to leave the Sound, incompetency of officers being freely charged, as well as that the boilers were leaking so badly when the ill-starred cruise was commenced that no fireman could work around them without being scalded.

"The matter is to be made the subject of a formal report, with a request that criminal proceedings be initiated."

Other rumors said Captain Lewis had asked to be released from his command at Juneau but had been refused.

In Seattle, the disaster prompted even greater controversy, populist publisher Col. Alden J. Blethen, according to the *H.W. McCurdy History of the Pacific Northwest*, brutally wielding his *Times* editorials against the Republican administration's steamboat inspection service.

"...The wail of anguish that went up from the doomed throng aboard the boat that night and the sighs of grief that today break forth from the broken hearts of those whose loved ones were on the boat have found an echo in the hearts of all who have learned of this disaster, and in their indignation they will not rest appeased until those responsible for this terrible crime have been brought to justice and adequately punished.

"Once more, the *Times* demands that the inspectors speak. You, Mr. (C.C.) Cherry, and you, Mr. (W.J.) Bryant. You, who permitted that vessel to leave this port — what have you to say? The public want to know. The children, wives and mothers of those who were so suddenly ushered into eternity because you appear to have neglected your sworn duties want to know.

"Speak, men, speak, or else by your moody silence you admit that there is some foundation for the odious suspicions now hurled toward you by the public whom you once swore to serve faithfully and well. Have you fulfilled that oath?"

An opposition newspaper, the *Post-Intelligencer,* immediately leaped to the inspectors' defence, publishing expert opinion that the boilers had not exploded and glowing testimonials of prominent marine men as to the character and competency of *Nevada's* officers and crew. In answer to the charges of drunkenness among the company, the *Intelligencer* stated the mishaps at Seattle and Port Townsend were the result of a broken engineroom telegraph cable.

Probably the height—or depth—of the weeks-long *Times* onslaught was the editorial which challenged Inspectors Cherry and Bryant to forward a defence like "decent criminals!" The same account suggested a "fair trial," followed by the aforementioned officials "decorat(ing) the end of an elevated rope!"

Accusation and counter charge had been so fast and furious that, today, it is difficult if not impossible to learn the full truth. However, when all is said and done, it appeared ancient *Clara Nevada* had been sunk by explosion, although not that of her boilers.

The new theory, advanced by subsequent examination of the wreck, indicated she had been wrecked when fire swept through a cargo of blasting powder, carried from Puget Sound "in defiance of regulations forbidding the handling of explosives by passenger steamers.

"The *Stikine River Journal* asserts that the hull of the lost vessel, now lying in 12 feet of water, shows little damage amidships where the boilers were placed, while the entire stern is gone, and the wreck is badly shattered aft, otherwise that it is certain the force of the explosion was here severest. This theory, it is pointed out, coincides perfectly with the description of the explosion by the people of Seward City, who said there was a crash, a great sheet of flame leaping skyward, and immediately after, all was clear."

This theory of fire followed by horrendous blast was virtually confirmed when the divers reported fire hose coupled to the ship's pumps and laid along her sunken decks. Whether her maligned boilers started the blaze will never be known.

But the tragedy of the *Clara Nevada* was by no means ended, as readers of Washington's most entertaining nautical writer, Gordon R. Newell, will be aware. Seventeen years ago, in his popular *SOS North Pacific,* Newell recounted the eerie "death and resurrection" of the *Nevada.* It had been in 1908, he wrote that yet another storm had swept Lynn Canal's length, as the lightkeeper at Elder Rock had listened to the banshee winds which shook his perch high above the rocks and waves.

All that night the storm had blustered until, finally, the worst had passed and, with dawn, the lightkeeper had ventured outside. However, what had begun as a routine inspection of the island soon became an exercise in horror, as, when he reached the rocky promontory's northern tip, he had been unable to believe his eyes. For there, driven high and dry by the gale, had been the shattered hulk of the *Clara Nevada!*

Incredibly, the ghost had been real enough, being complete with the ill-fated ship's company; then no more than bones among the debris and marine growth...

Clara Nevada's doomed hundred were the victims of the age in which they lived; the hectic day when dreams of raw gold drew men from every corner of the globe in anything that would float, forsaking comfort and safety in their mad rush to the diggings. Considering the majority of craft pressed into service, and the notoriety of British Columbian and Alaskan shores, it can only be marvelled that most, if not all, did not meet with tragedy.

Chapter 15

Death Rode The Waves

Almost all Pacific Northwest ports fell victim as one shipping mishap occurred after another, a century ago. But none was as staggering or as controversial as the wreck of the ancient steamer *Pacific,* but hours after she cleared Victoria, November 4, 1875.

This appalling disaster — only two of more than 250 persons survived — is one of the worst in West Coast history. But the *Pacific's* loss is vividly remembered because, as she went down, the sturdy vessel which rammed her mysteriously sailed on, leaving hundreds of men, women and children to perish...

Much reference has been made to this tragedy over the years. But the original puzzle remains. *How,* even in the perilous days of sail a century ago, could such an accident occur?

One important factor was the *Pacific* herself. Said the *Colonist:* "Built about 25 years since to supply a sudden demand for shipping in the California trade, she was not considered a safe boat 17 years ago when Captain Wright ran her in the Oregon and Vancouver Island trade; and steamers, it is well known, do not, like wine, improve with age...

"We earnestly hope that as this terrible visitation has sealed the doom of nearly 100 (sic) human beings, it will also mark the close of the era of 'floating coffins' and 'rotten tubs' in the North Pacific. It is appalling to reflect that between a passenger and instant destruction there is but a thin plank. But when that plank is rotten as well as thin...!"

Few of the happy hundreds who pressed aboard the aging steamer could have appreciated her sorry condition. Families, miners and Chinese laborers lining her rails expected nothing beyond safe,

100

uneventful passage "below" to San Francisco. They probably did not even realize that she was dangerously overloaded — some passengers even had climbed over the rail as the gangplank was removed.

Ss. *Pacific* struggled from Victoria at 9:30 on the morning of November 4. That night, she met her dreadful fate off Cape Flattery. But it was not until four days later that Victorians learned of the calamity. A special edition of the *Colonist* gave the few details then known. In a grim editorial, the saddened editor wrote: "The catastrophe is so far-reaching that scarcely a household in Victoria but has lost one or more of its members, or must strike from its list of living friends a face and form that found ever a warm greeting within their circle.

"A bolt out of the blue could not have caused more widespread consternation... In some cases entire families have been swept away. In others, fond wives...have gone down to an early grave. In others, the joyous, happy maiden; the sweet, innocent prattling babe; the banker, the merchant, the miner, the public officer — all have found a common grave..."

Pacific had passed Tatoosh Light late in the afternoon, fighting a heavy swell and strong wind. Six hours later, when the collision occurred, the tired coaster was but 20 miles from shore. Most passengers were asleep when the sudden crash sent them crowding on deck. The following nightmare is best described by one of her two survivors, quartermaster Neil Henley.

Henley had finished his watch at 8 p.m. and retired below, when the *Pacific* shuddered under impact. Jumping from his bunk, he found "water rushing into the hold at a furious rate. On reaching the deck all was confusion. I looked on the starboard beam and saw a large vessel under sail, which they said had struck the steamer... The captain and officers were trying to lower the boats but the passengers crowded in against their commands, making their efforts useless. There were 15 women and six men in the boat with me, but she struck the ship and filled instantly, and when I came up I caught hold of a skylight, which soon capsized..."

While aboard the stricken *Pacific,* Henley had helped launch one lifeboat, then assisted in lowering another. The first splintered against the *Pacific's* hull, crushing a baby which had been placed in the boat by its mother, and drowning the other occupants. Henley jumped into the second craft, but it "was so crammed with people she could not be rowed; I think the boat was damaged by coming against the ship, as I found she was half-full of water immediately afterward."

It was then that he struck out on his own, swimming to the steamer's floating hurricane deck. When he looked for the ship, she had disappeared. Already clinging to the crowded hurricane deck were Captain J.D. Howell, second mate A. Wells, a cook, another quartermaster, and three passengers, including a woman...

Captain Howell's career had been an exciting one. Brother-in-law of Confederate President Jefferson Davis, he had been imprisoned with his famous relative after a gallant role in the rebel navy. Later returning to the sea, he had skippered several coastal steamers. Shortly before his last command, his ship, the *Los Angeles,* had wrecked off Tillamook Head. After "encountering unnumbered perils, he reached the land and brought intelligence of the disaster to Astoria."

Now he and his drenched companions shivered on their tiny float. *Pacific* had gone down; no lifeboats were to be seen. Screams of the drowning haunted them in the darkness — then silence. The phantom ship which had struck *Pacific* her death blow sailed on into the night.

Then, said Henley, it was all over; the cries had ceased, and he and his companions were alone on the raft.

Following is his heartrending account of the ordeal aboard a piece of wreckage, as the sea stole his comrades one by one: "At 1 a.m. the sea was making a clean breach over the raft. At 4 a.m. a heavy sea washed over us, carrying away the captain, second mate, the lady and another passenger, leaving four of us... At 9 a.m. the cook died and rolled off into the sea."

The hours passed, the hardships increased. Late the following afternoon, "the mist cleared away, and we saw land about 15 miles away. We also saw a piece of wreckage with two men on it. At 5 p.m. another man expired, and early the next morning the other one died, leaving me alone. Soon after the death of the last man I caught a floating box and dragged it on (to) the raft. It kept the wind off, and during the day I slept considerable."

Early on the morning of November 8, four days after the disaster, Henley was picked up by the revenue cutter *Oliver Wolcott.* The haggard seaman suffered from exposure, shock, hunger and exhaustion. But he was alive.

Only one other survivor was found, passenger Henry F. Jelley having lashed himself to the *Pacific's* pilothouse, which had been torn loose when the steamer sank. Rescued two days later by the bark *Messenger,* he first said *Pacific* struck a rock south of Cape Flattery.

Rushed to port, he aroused the hopes of the crowds lining Victoria docks, waiting for word of missing relatives and friends. Jelley thought the two lifeboats had been safely launched...

A small fleet of rescue vessels immediately sailed in search of other survivors. Hundreds continued to wait and to pray at the waterfront for information. When the steamer *Gussie Telfair* docked in the evening of November 10, the pier was alight with lanterns and torches. The anxious crowd pressed forward, asking those aboard for any news. A deckhand wearily replied: "We've got two men and a woman, dead, and no one else."

"It seemed as if all Victoria had gathered there to mourn," reported the *Colonist*. "Before the boat was made fast the eager throng passed over the guards and rushed back to the spot where three narrow, mound-like something (sic) covered with tarps showed that there lay the remains of three human beings who, with 300 (sic) others, full of life and energy, sailed away from this port a few days before . . ."

The last body, that of a 25-year-old woman, was "scanned . . . for a trace of resemblance to some loved one known to have been on board the ill-fated ship." Silently, hundreds passed the tiny form, none able to say, "That was my daughter, or my wife, or my sister, who was lost in the *Pacific*." All shook their heads and turned away. Suddenly, a "prominent citizen" rushed forward and identified her. The crowd rejoiced, finding some satisfaction in the fact that she had been claimed.

In following days, more bodies and wreckage were found. A shattered rowboat drifted ashore near Victoria's Clover Point. A grimmer discovery was the body of attractive Fanny Palmer, 19, who had sailed aboard the *Pacific* to join her sisters in San Francisco; her remains floating ashore almost at the very doorstep of her home.

The body of gold commissioner John Howe Sullivan was found at Becher Bay by Indians. He was interred at Ross Bay Cemetery.

To date, nothing had been heard of the phantom sailing ship which had nudged the *Pacific* on that fateful night. No one knew her identity or her whereabouts, and all prayed that she would soon dock with survivors. On November 16, the ghastly facts swept Victoria. Shocked and enraged, the city was in an uproar.

For it had been learned that the mysterious culprit was the American sailing vessel *Orpheus,* Captain Charles A. Sawyer commanding. Ironically, *Orpheus* herself had become a total loss off Cape Beale, the morning after her collision with the *Pacific*. No *Pacific* survivors were aboard her.

The common belief that Captain Sawyer callously sailed away, leaving hundreds struggling in the sea, fanned the entire Northwest into "lynch fever." Even today it is acknowledged that, "so strong was this sentiment that he would have undoubtedly met with severe treatment had he been in the city (Victoria) at that time."

The coroner's inquest at Victoria sternly condemned the officers of both the *Pacific* and the *Orpheus*, charging that the former's lifeboat capacity could handle but half her human cargo, that she was in deplorable condition, and that her lookout had been insufficient. *Orpheus,* it ruled, had "unjustifiably" crossed *Pacific's* bow, and Captain Sawyer had not remained by the sinking steamer "to ascertain the damage she had sustained."

Sawyer then was arrested in San Francisco on the charge he had deliberately cast *Orpheus* away. Acquitted of that absurdity, he found

103

himself bitterly denounced and hated the length of the West Coast. Then his crew formally accused him of having deliberately deserted the *Pacific* — despite his having heard the screams of the dying.

At the official inquiry in the Bay City, Sawyer testified that his second mate had mistaken Pacific's riding lights for the Cape Flattery lighthouse. Due to the heavy seas, his deck watch had not spotted the lights until they were almost onto the *Pacific* and it was too late.

". . . She blew her whistle," recalled Sawyer, "and immediately struck us on the starboard side in the wake of the main hatch. The blow was a light one. She had evidently stopped her engines and was backing and gave us a glancing blow, for she bounced off and again struck us at the main topmast backstays, breaking the chain plates."

Pacific had struck him again, he said, leaving him "comparatively a wreck on the starboard side." When his crew had rushed to their emergency stations, they found *Orpheus* to be half-full of water, and Sawyer had set about repairing his ship, which engaged his attention "10 to 15 minutes." He said he had been too busy during this time to look to the steamer. Once safely underway, he had looked back. But nothing was to be seen or heard. His men then commenced to berate the other vessel, he said, for not having seen to their injuries . . .

The court finally granted Sawyer the benefit of the doubt. He was widely respected (at least, up until this time) although a hard master; a trait which was thought to be the motive of his crewmen in trying to destroy him with their accusations. But the world was not as forgiving. Until his death in 1894, Captain Sawyer was cursed for having abandoned *Pacific's* company to their deaths.

Several attempts have been made in recent years to salvage the *Pacific's* safe, containing a Wells Fargo shipment of $79,220 in currency and gold. Many of her passengers had been miners returning from the Cassiar, and it is thought that their wealth makes the *Pacific* worth $200,000 to the lucky finder. However, the sketchy details known of her tragic end have made pinpointing her exact location extremely difficult, although in 1961 American skin-divers claimed to have recovered several relics from her rotting hulk.

Captain Charles A. Sawyer died 20 years after the notorious shipwreck, a very lonely man. For many years, it was reported, he had not dared to visit Victoria where feelings continued to run high against him. In fact, in the weeks immediately following the collision, he had been forced to hide in the home of the Port Townsend collector of customs. Upon news of his passing, in 1894, the *Colonist* noted: "Captain Sawyer in later years suffered much from the recollections of the sad event. An incident occurred not long ago in Port Townsend that aptly illustrates his peace of mind. He was visiting a neighbor one evening, the conversation lagged, and he was gazing intently into the glowing grate for several minutes and then suddenly exclaimed:

'There, I heard the whistle plainly.' In explanation he said he could hear distinctly the *Pacific's* whistle, and that it was a constant worriment to his peace of mind . . ."

Whether or not Captain Sawyer earned the resentment that followed him to his grave remains another mystery of the Pacific Northwest.

Chapter 16

A Killer Wave Took Little Velos

A violent sou'easter was raking Victoria when the little tug *Velos* and her heavy barge crept from the outer harbor.

In her pitching wheelhouse on that wild night of March 22, 1895, Captain Anderson and his mate, Andrew Christensen, anxiously watched the wildy-snaking hawser between their tiny steamer and bucking tow.

Aboard the old *Pilot,* astern, were 24 worried men. Once a Columbia River bar tug, *Pilot* had been stripped to her hull for hauling limestone and workers from up-Island quarries. Now she struggled in the *Velos'* wake.

Suddenly Christensen yelled, "Cap'n I think she's going to hit us!"

Spinning the wheel hard over, Anderson could see the barge over his shoulder, as it rocketed out of the gloom on a towering wave and descended upon their lurching counter . . .

Captain Anderson had had difficulties all evening. He intended to clear Victoria by 6:30 p.m., but three hours were lost before his crew rounded up all of the workers slated to board the *Pilot* for Haddington and Nelson Islands. By then, the wind was screaming from the southeast. Although Anderson was reluctant to leave port, his schedule called for prompt delivery of his passengers, and he grimly cast off.

Also aboard the tug was 55-year-old contractor Frederick Adams, who had chartered *Velos* and *Pilot* to carry limestone for the provincial legislative buildings, then under construction. Oddly, he had written his will that very morning.

Velos' crew comprised chief engineer Arthur Bloor; his assistant, William Law; deckhand French Duncan (a former law student whose great grandfather, Dr. Henry Duncan, pioneered today's banking system), and Robert ("Soda Water Bob") Smith, cook . . .

The 49-ton cannery and towing veteran had to fight for every inch of progress. As the lights of harbor fell astern, the March gale caught her full on the starboard bow, driving her ever closer to shore and destruction. More than an exhausting hour passed before Captain Anderson sighted Trial Island ahead.

Her little steam engine wheezed asthmatically as it strained against wind and tide, Anderson having decided to worry his charge into Cadboro Bay and to await daylight.

But *Velos* did not make it. As she struggled through Enterprise Channel, between Trial Island and Oak Bay, the storm struck her full force. It was all Anderson could do to keep her bow into the wind. His eyes found those of Christensen, who nodded to his unspoken question.

"Aye, bring her about, Cap'n . . ."

Groaning, old *Velos* entered her turn, the yawning *Pilot* almost crippling her manoeuvrability. Whenever the wind fell off, the barge would charge its stalled escort, threatening to sink her in collision, then would snap backward as another gust caught her like a sail. And once again the former tug would strain against poor *Velos*.

It was as the tug grudgingly angled about that disaster struck. A giant wave caught her broadside, swept over her decks and swamped her. With a grinding crash, she splintered against the island reefs.

"The steamer went 'round on the port, the helm hard over, and we were making to clear the point of rocks when the wheel chains carried away," Christensen later reported.

"If they had held another minute, and we could have cleared the point, we might have gone through, but where we were they had no sooner gone than the *Velos* went 'round broadside to the wind and a heavy sea swept over and swamped her. It would have done no good to reverse the engine even if we had time to — and we hadn't."

When the killing wave struck, only Christensen and Frank Duncan were on deck. Captain Anderson was at the helm, contractor Adams in the galley, engineers Bloor and Law at their stations below decks, and cook Smith in his cabin.

Christensen, whose brother James had been lost at sea but months before, had just inspected the towline when Velos shuddered under the impact. Sensing the gravity of her injuries, he ran to the boats in a desperate bid to clear them before *Velos* filled, when they were swept from their davits.

Glancing up, he saw the *Pilot* descending upon him "like a steam engine, and I knew that if she struck us she would go clear through!"

Just as a collision seemed inevitable, the *Pilot* careened into a submerged rock and sheered off. The sudden strain whipped the towline above water, offering Christensen his chance.

Shouting the alarm to his comrades, he monkied up the coiling line.

As tension between the vessels eased, he plummetted into the surf, then was snapped upwards as another sea heaved *Pilot* away from her consort. The hawser jarred bones, seared bare palms and fingers...

Somehow he reached *Pilot's* side and was immediately pulled to temporary safety by those aboard, who had watched his frantic retreat. When seaman Frank Duncan tried following, *Pilot's* company could only shout encouragement; they were powerless. Desperately gripping the tossing line, Duncan wormed his way forward. Then a large wave crashed over him and he was gone.

By now, only part of *Velos'* bow and wheelhouse remained above water. Adams had been trapped in the galley. Engineer Bloor and cook Smith tried swimming for the nearby, but invisible, shore. They vanished in the surf.

Captain Anderson and engineer Law continued to cling to the wreck for dear life. Awash, freezing and terrified, they held fast to their precarious perch for an hour. Then, sure that he could not hold on much longer, Anderson resolved to swim. Taking a deep breath, he struck out into the darkness, grabbing for air until, finally, he felt jagged stone ahead and pulled himself upward.

Legs cut and bruised, head bleeding, Anderson gingerly explored his tiny "anchorage." In despair, he found that he was on a ledge somewhere in the channel — a long way from land. Then unconsciousness gave him brief respite from his ordeal . . .

Meanwhile, the *Pilot's* frightened crew were experiencing their own drama.

In fact, the 25 men on the barge has less chance of survival than those aboard the tug. The *Velos* at least had had propulsion; the *Pilot* was a floating hulk, victim of the gale's every whim. Her passengers could see nothing in the raging blackness, could do nothing but wait and pray. Buffetted by wind, the *Pilot* crashed into one reef after another, opening seams, splitting planks. She was yet hooked to the *Velos*, the sunken tug acting as an anchor.

Then the hawser pulled free, wrenching the capstan from *Velos'* submerged stern, and *Pilot* drifted with the rip tides. Her passengers could hear the others crying for help above the storm.

Recognizing Law's voice, mate Christensen and several men tried to launch the barge's lifeboat. As soon as the flimsy craft touched water, it smashed against *Pilot's* hull and was ruined.

Miraculously, the barge drifted, stern-first, into a tiny Trial Island cove — driving aground at the one place where the rocks would not rip out her weakened bottom. There, the haggard survivors waited for dawn, nerves frayed by the agonized cries of their hapless companions. Four voices could be heard at first, then only two. They shouted back, urging Captain Anderson and Law not to give up.

It was their calling that kept Anderson alive, he admitted later, explaining that he could not have continued the struggle had he not known that they were nearby and thinking of him.

Poor Law's voice grew steadily weaker. Again and again he cried, first in the direction of shore, where he could not be heard, then to the others, who could not reach him: "Won't someone *please* help me!"

Eventually they heard him no more.

When the winds slackened, they lowered a plank to the beach and searched the island with lanterns. They found no bodies but, in a former hermit's cabin, they discovered food, blankets and firewood. With dawn, they again scoured the island, finding *Velos'* two lifeboats washed ashore. Both were battered but, with bailing and patching, one was sufficiently repaired so as to rescue Captain Anderson.

Anderson huddled before a fire, swathed in blankets, while the others searched for wreckage and tried signalling to passing vessels. They finally flagged a fishboat, which took one of the workers to Victoria with the news. They need not have worried. Previously, a Foul Bay resident had flashed the alarm, after seeing them on the island and debris littering the waves.

Captain John Irving immediately ordered his steamer *Maude* to the scene, leading the rescue party himself. The sight that greeted him on Trial Island shocked even that veteran. Each of the 26 survivors was drenched, many of them half-naked, most without shoes. All were exhausted.

Irving then inspected poor *Velos*, of which only her bow and mast were visible. A grimmer discovery was Law's body, floating on the surface, one foot caught in the tug's rigging. With his foot trapped, he had struggled to remain above the rising tide, until it had drowned him.

Tragically, Law had obtained his berth on the doomed *Velos* but a short time before, having been ill for eight months previous.

Flag at half-mast, *Maude* returned to Victoria.

A later examination showed that the *Velos'* entire bottom had fallen out, spilling her machinery and boilers onto the seabed. The *Pilot* was salvaged. Ashore, hundreds of volunteers paced the beaches and navigated small boats in quest of the four missing men.

Days later, a coroner's inquiry heard mate Christensen's account of the tragedy, as Captain Anderson remained in critical condition in Royal Jubilee Hospital.

From New Westminster, W. E. Duncan arrived to aid in the search for his brother's body. Earlier, Frank's coat had been found in the wreckage of the collier *San Pedro,* whose bones still lie in the gloomy depths off Brotchie Ledge, where she grounded in 1891. It was believed that Duncan had removed his coat so as to try swimming to safety.

In the meantime, word was sent to cook Robert Smith's aged

mother in England. His only relative, she had depended upon a monthly allowance he sent her for living expenses.

Sons of contractor Frederick Adams refuted the rumors their father had been carrying large sums of money at the time of his death, saying that he could have had no "more than $50 or $60 at the most." They offered $100 for recovery of his body.

The entire city took up a collection for engineer William Law's destitute widow and her three small children. The local militia offered a public show which included a band concert and various drills, the proceeds of which were given to Mrs. Law. Within two days, almost $200 had been collected for the bereaved family.

Three-quarters of a century after the *Velos* met her fate off Trial Island (a lighthouse was established there in 1906), an article in a Victoria newspaper concerning the old Adams home on Pembroke Street mentioned that, on that fateful morning of March 23, 1895, the contractor's family had been gathered in the drawing room. When, suddenly, their dog began to howl, Mrs. Adams reputedly gasped that something had happened to her husband. Also, apparently, each of the men's pocket watches had stopped at 2 a.m.

Chapter 17

Carelmapu: *Last Windjammer To Die In Pacific Graveyard*

The last windjammer to be claimed by Vancouver Island's murderous Graveyard of the Pacific drove ashore during the violent night of November 25, 1915.

With dawn, it was all over. The once proud three-master *Carelmapu* was awash, her back broken, most of her crew swept away.

"All hands lost off West Coast," cried *Colonist* headlines on the morning of November 26. Details were sketchy, as hurricane-force winds had downed all telephone and telegraph lines near Tofino. Days before, Victorians had read of the total loss of the steamer *Idaho* near Prince Rupert.

The beautiful Chilean square-rigger was out of Honolulu, bound in ballast for Puget Sound, when she reached the entrance to moody Juan de Fuca Strait. As was customary, 31-year-old Captain Fernando Desolmes signalled for a tow.

Upon checking his barometer, he found it to be falling rapidly. A storm was approaching and his 38-year-old ship was in an exposed position. Realizing the gravity of his situation, the skipper quickly ordered her about and sailed for the Swiftsure Lightship, where he would ride out the gale until a tug came for him.

He could not know that the Northwest had been plagued by severe storms for days and that no help was coming...

The sou'wester broke, pounding *Carelmapu* viciously. Riding light before the 40-knot winds, she rolled dangerously in the towering seas that swept across her decks and edged her closer to shore. Captain Desolmes had shortened sail, but the wind scissored through the canvas until only shreds flapped impotently from her lofty masts.

It was as his men scrambled up the slippery rigging to bend new sails that the cry, "Land O!" warned of a newer, greater danger.

Hours later, the battered *Carelmapu* was still caught in the gale and laboring heavily. Near frantic with the helplessness of his plight, Captain Desolmes took a sounding: 240 fathoms. Unable to escape the wind-whipped currents pushing him ever closer to the rocks, he ordered both anchors dropped. Every man aboard held his breath as the heavy chains reeled out, praying that the anchors would take hold. A sudden lurch, a groan, and *Carelmapu* paused; her anchors gripping the seabed.

Just a cable-length away—the rocky beach.

Aware that he could not trust his anchors, Desolmes ordered several crewmen into a lifeboat. The sailors struggled over submerged decks, which were now constantly awash, and worried a reluctant boat over the side. Upon their clambering in, the craft began its descent, when a terrified seaman lost his grip of the forward line, and the lifeboat plunged seaward, bow-first, and catapaulted its occupants into the surf. Some were sucked under instantly, others crushed against the *Carelmapu's* steel hull as the empty boat disintegrated in pounding waves...

That afternoon, the coastal steamer *Princess Maquinna* chanced upon the scene during her last West Coast run of the season. Veteran skipper Captain Edward Gillam quickly appraised the situation, later describing the storm as the worst he had experienced.

But *Maquinna* was young and strong. Destined to faithfully serve isolated Island communities for 40 years, thus earning the affectionate title, Old Faithful, *Maquinna* then was but two-years-old. Had she not been new and the finest ship to sail these troubled waters, she would have joined *Carelmapu* on the reef.

Captain Gillam's first responsibility was to his passengers, however. Even before sighting *Carelmapu,* he had considered returning to port. In fact, he said later, he had had a premonition that "something was going to happen." But he had full confidence in his ship. Skilfully manoeuvring the *Maquinna* to within 150 yards of the Chilean, he intended getting a line aboard the *Carelmapu* and tow her into deep water. Whether he seriously considered salvage possible is a moot point.

A stout hawser snaked towards the square-rigger, and splashed into the sea. Gillam had missed. The violence of the seas spoiled the most experienced aim and Gillam would have to think of something else—fast.

But he was powerless.

The crewmen hugging *Maquinna's* bucking railings watched tensely as the last act unfolded aboard the South American. They could do nothing but wait and hope for the best, as their own ship strained at full speed so as to ease the pressure on her anchors. Jettisoned oil calmed the seas somewhat, but not enough...

Those remaining aboard the *Carelmapu* had watched in horrified fascination as their comrades had vanished when their lifeboat was upset. Now it was their turn, and in terror and futile anger they cursed the overpowering sea which held them in its deathly grip. Then seven men forced another boat overboard and climbed in.

This time, they succeeded in clearing *Carelmapu's* side without incident, and rowed desperately for nearby *Maquinna*. Gillam launched a line, attached to a float, in the hope that it would drift to them. But a giant wave capsized the boat, throwing its occupants into the sea. All drowned.

Then the storm turned its full attention upon the *Carelmapu*, whose anchors valiantly fought to keep her from the rocks. With a scream of tortured, twisted metal, a chain snapped. *Carelmapu* pivoted about on her remaining anchor, her stern slamming into a reef. The dying ship sagged onto its beam, the impact knocking more men into the sea.

The gust that delivered the *Carelmapu's* death blow also did its best to wreck the *Maquinna*. Yawing against her anchor cables when the wave struck, the sudden strain proved to be overwhelming. *Maquinna's* winches groaned, slipped, and gave. Bolts and cogs sheered off as the winches were jerked forward. But *Maquinna* was made of the best materials; her anchors budged slightly, then held once more.

This near-fatal mishap, however, convinced Captain Gillam that he was courting disaster. He could do nothing to help those aboard the *Carelmapu,* and his own ship and many passengers and crewmen were endangered. When he ordered the 60-fathom-long anchor chain hack-sawed free, *Maquinna* nosed seaward.

Several of his seamen had volunteered to launch a lifeboat. But Gillam knew that it was hopeless and demurred, believing the *Carelmapu* to be "gone and all hands." Hurrying to Ucluelet, he notified Tofino of the square-rigger's plight. But the lifeboat stationed there could not venture out in such weather, and the *Carelmapu* was on her own...

The Chilean's once-perpendicular mizzenmast now lay parallel to the breakers. Desperately, Captain Desolmes and two men pulled themselves along this slender bridge as the Pacific hungrily reached out for them. Beneath them, the storm ground *Carelmapu's* steel bottom across the reef like a giant seesaw, gutting her from bow to stern. Suddenly the windjammer cracked in half, the bow sinking. When the mizzenmast shattered, two feet from the deck, Desolmes and companions were sent sprawling into the water.

Blinded and choked by the salt spray attacking his eyes, nose and mouth, Desolmes fought clear of the collapsed masts and rigging that filled the seas like a drunken net. For 30 minutes, he struggled to remain afloat, when at last his feet touched land. As he lunged for the shore, the undertow jerked him backward. Again and again, this agonizing drill was repeated: the sea sadistically allowing him to touch land, only to pluck him back once more.

The fourth time, Desolmes' clawing fingers found a grip; some logs littering the beach. His feet, lacerated almost beyond recognition by the rocks, touched shore, and he was safe.

Others also reached land: young Spaniard Rodrigo Diez, enroute to study at the University of Washington, and three more. Diez's friend, Claudio Urutia, also a student, died in the wreck. Of *Carelmapu's* company of 24, Diez, Desolmes, two seamen—and the ship's dog— were all who survived.

Finding each other in the dark, they searched for shelter. Luckily, they came upon a deserted Indian shack and gratefully piled in. All were battered and drenched, some left almost naked by the surging currents. Huddled in their little refuge, they massaged each other to restore circulation and drive away their new enemy, cold.

Long hours after, one exclaimed: "I heard voices. Listen!"

They had been found by rescuers who had trekked from Tofino and Clayoquot with food and medical supplies. After eating, their strength somewhat restored, the marooned seamen helped their rescuers search for more survivors. Two bodies were found, their clothing being recovered, dried over a fire, and given to the shivering seamen.

They then located another survivor, wandering dazedly along the beach, and maddened by his ordeal. He wore heavy clothing and a lifebelt but had no shoes, and his feet had been mutilated by rocks and brush. He had to be forcibly restrained from re-entering the water.

Escorted to Long Beach, the survivors were nursed by settler H.P. Cooper and his wife. The storm had abated, and the Tofino lifeboat crew took them to Clayoquot, where they boarded the ship which had so valiantly tried to save them, *Princess Maquinna*. The *Carelmapu's* dog chose to remain with the Coopers, living with them for several years until "eventually shot by a souvenir hunter for the brass plate on his collar."

The lifeboat then journeyed to the wreck, when six bodies were recovered and buried nearby. The seamen boarded *Carelmapu's* amputated stern, still perched high on the rocks, and salvaged documents, equipment and personal effects belonging to the survivors. Years later, salvors obtained much of her steel for wartime manufacturing.

Ironically, said Captain Gillam of the *Maquinna*, if he had "known of the vessel being in distress two hours earlier it would have been possible to save all on board the *Carelmapu,* as there would have been plenty of room to manoeuvre outside the breakers..."

Other ships suffered in the storm which wrecked *Carelmapu,* the

Japanese steamer *Sado Maru* limping into port after a close call when her steering gear had been knocked out of commission for three days.

In recent years a Tofino resident visited the square-rigger's grave and recovered a "dead-eye" from her rigging as a souvenir. Parts of the wreck, he said, were still visible at extremely low tide. He also noted the ship's winch, parts of her masts, and "Several other identifiable parts." Another Tofino resident is known to possess Captain Desolmes' sword and "several other articles" which were given to the Coopers years before.

A third Tofino man, although only 12-years-old at the time, vividly recalled "that terrible day." His father and two uncles helped provincial police bury *Carelmapu's* dead; those that were recovered.

Thirty-five years before the *Carelmapu,* the San Francisco vessel *General Cobb* wrecked in almost the same spot under identical circumstances. Fortunately for the Americans, none were lost as local Indians rescued and cared for them.

Many other shipwrecks dot this lethal stretch of Vancouver Island's west coast.

Chapter 18

Swiftwater Horror

It took more than skill to be eligible for the pioneer British Columbia order of mariners known as swiftwater pilots—it took sheer guts.

Besides the innumerable death-traps of raging currents—not to mention boilers which exploded with almost monotonous regularity—a riverboat skipper had to contend with the competition. Rules of the road were open to interpretation; should a master choose to argue the right-of-way, it was every boat for itself and heaven protect the passengers!

Although this rambunctious breed, which opened B.C.'s hinterland to gold-hungry prospectors from 1858 onward, had become respectable by the turn of the century, there was still the odd throwback to wilder days. Men like fiery Captain J. H. Bonsar, onetime master of the Steamer *Hazelton*, who was hauled before a special board of inquiry in Victoria to answer charges laid by another Skeena River master, Captain Stewart B. Johnson.

It seems Captain Bonsar objected to Johnson's new sternwheeler, the popular *Mount Royal*, sharing the same river—to the point of shifting a navigation buoy. Captain Johnson not unnaturally drew the nasty conclusion Bonsar hoped he would crack up his ship.

Passengers told hair-raising tales of races between the two steamers. If either paused to load wood, and the rival craft steamed into view, deckhands would clamber aboard, cut the moorings and the battle was on. Speedy *Mount Royal* invariably took the honors. Not that Captain Bonsar could be accused of not trying.

Once, witnesses testified, the *Hazelton* had been loading wood at Hardscrabble Bar when the Hudson's Bay Company steamer chanced upon the scene. Hastily slipping his lines, Captain Bonsar had boiled across stream to the port channel.

"The *Mount Royal* gained quickly . . . and with her engines thumping noisily made her way past the bow of the *Hazelton*. But Captain Bonsar would not be beaten. The bow of his vessel struck the (*Royal*) on her starboard quarter, pressing against her and swinging her around.

"As the *Hazelton* continued to push the after quarter, the *Royal* veered until she was broadside to the current. Gradually the *Hazelton* slid free, and the rival steamer, unable to answer her helm, was backed astern that she might be straightened up to the swift current again."

Bonsar had just begun to fight. Throwing his helm hard over, he was soon leading another attack, steaming full speed into the *Royal's* midriff; "it seemed as though one of the vessels was to be crippled!"

Shoving open his pilothouse window, Bonsar shook his fist angrily at Johnson, who shouted back, then ran to his cabin for his rifle! Their duel suddenly became near disaster as *Hazelton's* bow raked *Mount Royal's* tall superstructure and caught. The savage current then joined the melee, hurtling the entangled vessels shoreward.

Back at his post, Captain Johnson impotently spun the wheel, trying to regain control, but *Hazelton's* weight was too much, arching his ship about in a semi-circle. *Hazelton* then broke free; when with a defiant laugh and blast of his whistle, an elated Bonsar charged upstream and out of sight.

That was riverboating in British Columbia, 60 years ago!

For the record, it should be mentioned that Captain Johnson was of a somewhat different cut than the belligerent Bonsar. Then only 29, he was considered "one of the best river navigators and swiftwater masters on the Pacific Coast," having apprenticed on the busy freshwater steamers of Washington and Oregon.

The test of his skill and courage came without warning, two years later, on the bright summer afternoon of July 6, 1907.

Bound for Port Essington, at the mouth of the Skeena, *Mount Royal* cleared Hazelton on her last voyage at 9 a.m., July 6. ". . . In a few minutes," recalled passenger Edward Potts, "we were in the forks of the Skeena and Bulkley Rivers on a first-class and powerful steamer, commanded by an excellent, cool and calculating captain.

"There was very little freight on board, but that, unfortunately, was of considerable value. About 11 o'clock, we stopped for fuel and this took considerable time. Lunch was now served and the majority of us did justice to the same, and I fancy now I see Purser O'Keefe by my side, smiling, and Mate Lewis, with his quiet ways, aloft.

"A powerful blast of the whistle told us we were close to Meanskinisht, known to most travellers as the Holy City, and in charge of Rev. R. Tomlinson. Here we let off two prospectors and took on Miss A.L. Tomlinson, who is making her first trip outside in 19 years."

The voyage proceeded uneventfully until 3 o'clock, when "an extra long blast of the whistle announced we were going through (Kitselas) Canyon. O'keefe remarked to me that (the ship) had not touched a rock this year. At 3 p.m. by my watch, we entered the head, and O'Keefe said, 'Hold on tight, boys!' for a gust of wind had caught her bow and no one on earth could prevent the crash on the flat rock, throwing her bow up at least three feet."

Mount Royal had confidently barrelled into the mile-long gorge as she had so many times before during her busy five years. Captain Johnson caressed the large wheel as he deftly guided his surging craft through the hell of raging water known as Kitselas Canyon. Ringbolt Island, a long, low reef jutting up in mid-channel, began to flash by.

Swiftwater navigation was a delicate art; skill and nerves of steel against a vindictive foe. But even experience and courage could not cope with the unknown. Kitselas Canyon allowed not the slightest margin for error or the unexpected. When a squall knifed through the pass, it slammed the lightly-laden steamer's bluff housework like a fist.

High above, in the wheelhouse, Captain Johnson felt his ship shudder, as she nudged the island, even before he could think. *Mount Royal* groaned to a stop, her spoon-like bow impaled on the rocks. Almost by reflex, Johnson ordered the 27 passengers ashore and began bawling instructions to his crew to save the ship.

With Johnson directing operations from the wheelhouse, mate W.L. Lewis threw the gangplank overside and bundled the passengers, including Mrs. Johnson, onto the rocky island. There was no panic — indeed, hardly any haste — the passengers seemingly reluctant to abandon their comfortable ship for the inhospitable beach. All had been deceived by the light crash. They did not realize, as did the experienced crew, that time was their only ally. If *Mount Royal* could only be secured to the island, she might be saved.

Should the frothing Skeena regain control, the valiant steamer was doomed.

Calmly, the deckhands attempted to moor their stranded ship fore and aft to a tree. Lewis hoped to winch her snugly to the island, but found the capstan had been damaged and was useless. *Mount Royal's* precious minutes had run out.

Pivoting on her trapped bow, the ship began to spin towards the opposite shore. Slowly, then gaining speed as the current grabbed her, she whipped around. As the horrified passengers watched dazedly, the pride of the Skeena splintered her mightly paddlewheel against the other bank.

The steamer now was wedged cross-river like a dam!

The end came suddenly, violently. With her engineers and firemen at their post below, the deckhands at their emergency stations, Captain Johnson on the pilothouse roof, gallant *Royal* heeled before the overpowering fury of current and wind. The merciless river writhed over the starboard rail, flooding posh cabins, then with the strength of a tidal wave, shouldered her over.

To the gasps of those on shore, and the wail of straining, breaking wood and iron. *Mount Royal* turned turtle and started downstream, bottom up, at a murderous 10 knots.

Miraculously, Chief Engineer Bed Madigan and his assistant made their escape from below, reaching deck just as the steamer capsized. The frightened pair were instantly sucked away by the boiling current, remaining afloat by clutching pieces of wreckage.

"Their passage through the swirling waters must have been of the most thrilling character, and how they kept afloat is regarded as marvellous by those who know the awful speed of the waters of Kitselas Canyon. Their race against death lasted nearly a mile and it was when they had passed out of the canyon that they were able to make the shore."

Four hours later, the shivering engineers were rescued by Indians.

One of the Japanese deckhands had scrambled over the ship's rolling hull "like a squirrel in a revolving cage," to join three others on the wild voyage through the rapids on *Mount Royal's* bottom.

Bert Frayne, fireman, had been off watch at the time of the crash. He had helped passengers ashore and secured a hawser to the tree trunk, then hurried aboard to join his shipmates. He disappeared when the steamer rolled.

The heroic purser, Victorian James O'Keefe, had been first to help passengers disembark, then hastened back to the ship. He was last seen, by deckhand Joseph Offett, bravely swimming for shore. He vanished in a giant whirlpool. It would have been his 20th birthday the following Sunday.

Thirty-two-year-old steward Archie Willis and mate Lewis were last seen handling the lines on deck. When *Mount Royal's* shattered hulk drove aground on a sandbar downstream. Willis' mangled body was chopped from the wreckage.

After the passengers had been evacuated, "orders were given to throw out a cable and make fast to the island," recalled Offett. "This couldn't be done as the capstan had been damaged and put out of action. The mate ordered a cable on the after cleat to keep the boat from swinging. This was impossible, for the boat was tilting with each succeeding drop of water coming over her guard, and started to turn and tear herself away from the portion anchored on the ledge.

"I went over with the boat as she started down the waters of the rough canyon and landed below . . ." Entangled in the lifeboat when the ship overturned, the deckhand was dragged onto the hull by fireman William Jones. Steward Willis, he said, "was working with me on the cable and I did not see him again alive after the vessel tipped."

A passenger, Mrs. F. M. Phillips, of Oregon, told how purser O'Keefe had stormed into her stateroom, saying, "Quick, the boat is going to crack in 10 minutes!" and carried her ashore. He then returned to the ship and she "never saw him again."

Captain Johnson, she said, had "stepped down the companionway to the deck below and to the shore just as the *Royal* was turning." Johnson did not even wet his feet; a split second after he landed, *Mount Royal* capsized.

Throughout the disaster, Johnson had been "cool and collected," reported K. H. Rolley, a passenger from Matsqui. But when he saw "the best and most loyal crew that ever stepped on the deck of any boat" being whisked downstream, he "broke down and cried piteously . . . and the efforts of Edward Bissett and E. E. Potts, passengers, were necessary to keep him from jumping in the river."

Word of the tragedy reached Victoria almost instantly, government operator J. W. Graham, who manned a tidal gauge at the foot of Kitselas Canyon, telegraphing daily reports to Hazelton. He immediately wired the capital:

"*Mount Royal* total wreck in canyon 3 p.m. today; don't expect loss of life will be large as I can see a large crowd at Ringbolt Island, including the captain. First and second engineers came through canyon on debris. Indians in canoes are now working to get passengers off island. Expect to know full particulars at 7 p.m. — Graham."

The news "cast a shadow of gloom over the city," home of *Mount Royal's* six lost crewmen. As Skeena Indians courageously conducted the ticklish rescue of survivors stranded on Ringbolt Island, newspaper and telgraph offices were swamped by inquiries from anxious Victorians.

Lost Japanese deckhand Frank Amata had been an "interesting personality," and a veteran of the famous torpedo boat raids of the China-Japan war. "He knew every part of the *Mount Royal* and for general handiness was unsurpassed among the crew. He could turn his hands to carpentry and painting and was useful in many other respects. He was one of the most devoted servants of the company."

Sixth victim had been another Japanese, carpenter J. Morishima. During winter lay-up he and Amata had worked as waiters in the famous Pacific Club.

When all survivors had been attended to, Captain Johnson spent five days at the grim task of searching for bodies. Only Steward Willis' was found. Johnson dynamited river pools in hopes of driving bodies to the surface, but without success. Disheartened, he returned to Victoria.

A year before, the steamer *Pheasant* had wrecked in Kitselas Canyon without loss of life. Earlier, eight men had drowned in the deadly gorge when their barge overturned.

As we said, it took guts — and lots of them — to go riverboating in British Columbia way back when.

Chapter 19

Hera *Knew Infamy And Sorrow*

Strange are the tales of the sea; of phantom ships and ghostly crews; of wreck, horror and human endurance; of circumstances so uncanny as to defy belief—yet fully documented.

The Pacific Northwest has known its share of mysteries; the memory of one such tragedy was revived by skin-divers off the west coast of Vancouver Island in recent years.

In May of 1969, a Portland, Ore., expedition searching for the grave of the American fur trading ship *Tonquin,* shattered by explosion during Indian attack in 1811, located what appeared to be the remains of the ill-fated schooner *Hera* off Clayoquot Sound. Subsequent investigation revealed the wreck to be that of the barque *Coloma,* immortalized in Northwest marine lore by the courageous overland dash of British Columbia's "Grace Darling," Minnie Paterson.

But it is the *Hera* in which we are interested.

Boston-built in 1869, the 400-ton three-master had known adventure from the beginning. She looked like many sister craft which steadily plied the seas, challenging storm and reef to deliver varied cargoes. Yet *Hera* was to know more than the ordinary; she was to experience infamy and sorrow during her career of 30 years, and to die, unmourned, in Vancouver Island's graveyard of ships.

"Like a thief in the night, or a sheep-killing dog, afraid to face the light of day with honest men looking on, the piratical-looking craft crept past the city, silently and without noise . . ." Thus the *Hera's* arrival in Seattle in October, 1899, was recorded for posterity by the Seattle *Daily Times.*

Ships of every age, description and condition came and went

121

regularly during the hectic years of the Klondike craze, few exciting editorial comment beyond glowing descriptions of valuable cargoes. The bitter greeting for *Hera* came as the result of a terror-filled voyage from Nome; a voyage of which awed passengers spoke in hushed tones of the "dead, dying, crazed and crazy, weak, tottering and famishing."

It is difficult to comprehend, today, the dangers which passengers faced in going to sea, more than three-quarters of a century ago. The demand for shipping during the rush of 1897 saw dollar-hungry businessmen press every bottom into service. No matter that the hulk had rusted on a mudbank for years, that its timbers were almost transparent after too many years of hard service and neglect. As long as it floated — barely — and its patched boilers held enough steam to maintain headway, it was good enough to entrust hundreds of lives to one of the worst stretches of coastline braved by mariners.

Such was the fate of the *Hera*. She was old, she was tired — but she floated.

When the Blue Star Line's decrepit workhorse limped from Nome, her 200 passengers well knew that they were in for a rough passage; that, overloaded, undermanned and rotten, she promised nothing more than to reach her destination. Accommodation would be cramped and unsanitary, the food inadequate.

But, this time, of all the hazards facing the ancient veterans of the gold fleet, *Hera* faced yet another: starvation. For the food, guaranteed to be "all right, plenty of it, and wholesome and good," failed on all counts.

Within days, "meat, sugar and butter disappeared from the bill of fare. The meat consisted of salt horse and a limited supply of canned mutton. The supply of dried fruits seemed to consist from the first of only one box of dried peaches, enough to supply the tables with peaches three times, and prunes twice. As to potatoes, some of the passengers say that not a potato was seen aboard the ship. The only thing there seemed plenty of was flour. The ship never ran out of that, and the last four days the bill of fare was bread made from sourdough, and coffee."

To make matters worse, the salt horse "was counted a very poor quality by some of the passengers interviewed. Of this there was enough by rationing it to last up to four days ago, when the last of that commodity was gone. Then it was flour and water."

Then, even the water ran out, passengers being saved only by a providential rainfall.

For two of *Hera's* suffering company, relief came too late. J.S. Ryan of Sacramento withstood the ordeal for three weeks, as old *Hera* struggled southward. Weakened by malnutrition, exposure and inadequate ventilation, he had become delirious, wandering the cold decks in bare feet before sympathetic hands carried him below. Hours later, three weeks out, Ryan died and was buried at sea.

George Lamby soon followed, victim of malnutrition, typhoid and, it was charged, neglect.

Days passed, with Hera still far from port, delayed by opposing winds, and starvation faced surviving passengers who were on rations: dry bread and tepid coffee. Then there was no more coffee, as the ship was running low on water, until the welcome rains.

At last Hera raised Cape Flattery, passing word of her plight to the vessel Lakme, which instantly headed to port to notify authorities. Finally, the tug Sea Lion and cutter Grant steamed to the rescue, towing Hera into port after dumping meat, potatoes and other supplies upon the becalmed schooner's deck.

Upon anchoring in "the upper bay, close in against the foul-smelling fertilizer factory," Capt. J.L. Warren — "it certainly appeared as if he wanted to hide and have his arrival pass unnoticed" — abandoned his "famished and dying" passengers to get ashore as best they could.

Two months after her cruise as hellship, maligned Hera was again in the headlines. This time, newspapers recorded her obituary, the haunted schooner having been lost off Clayoquot.

Clearing Seattle, November 17, 1899, Captain Warren had proceeded only as far as Clallam Bay when forced to seek shelter, his rotten command threatening to buckle underfoot in the raging seas. Below her heaving decks was a general cargo which included everything from 750 barrels of beer to a prefabricated church. Also included were 1,800 barrels of lime.

When the weather cleared temporarily, Captain Warren headed into the Strait. But another gale descended, and aging Hera could take no more. Seams opened, flooding seas ignited the lime. And Hera was doomed.

For 24 terrifying hours, the schooner's frightened company had battled with pumps and hoses, inspired to remain at their posts by the encouraging words and smile of the purser, Miss Mabel Shirk. "No one could have a fear" in her presence, said mate J.A. McIntyre upon rescue.

With each passing hour, dying Hera was beaten closer to Vancouver Island and the unleashed monster below decks gained upon a retreating crew. Their only hope lay in reaching land before the fire broke free of its bonds.

When the schooner drifted into Clayoquot Sound, Warren dropped anchor, then, with Miss Shirk, her father, and two seamen, successfully launched the schooner's single boat, to row frantically for shore through mountainous waves, their bucking craft threatening to capsize with each blow. When they reached shore, a rescue team composed of Clayoquot settlers raced to the Hera's side to save her 13 remaining crewmen.

Captain Warren had intended returning for his panic-stricken crew until warned off by the rescue party who, upon reaching the blazing wreck, had faced an even greater danger: *Hera's* remaining company, terrified, lined her humping side, ready to leap into the lifeboat the instant that it came alongside. Realizing that this would swamp her and kill them all, one of the rescuers balanced himself against the plunging waves and raised an axe over his head, yelling that he would use it on the first man to jump.

It was rough diplomacy, but it worked, the seamen calming down immediately, when rescue proceeded without accident—although certainly not without incident.

When all were ashore, they had looked up, mouths agape in astonishment, as the eerie spectre, flames soaring skyward, phantom pilot at her helm, drifted easily through the rock-studded channel between Stubbs Island and Tofino. Steadily onward, past Felice Island, she followed the difficult course around island and through channel, until drifting ashore on the mudflats, ablaze from stem to stern.

So died the good schooner *Hera*. She had worked hard, suffered long. Never again would dying men curse her mythical name.

But if *Hera* was gone, she was not forgotten, newspapers recalling the Shakespearian tragedy in which she had played more than a decade earlier. For among the hundreds of hardy seamen who had slung their hammocks in the schooner's cramped fo'c'sle over the years, had been a young man who had called himself George Osborne. Faced roughened by years before the mast, he looked like any other able seaman of the age. If shipmates sensed a difference, it was only that he kept to himself.

But George Osborne was indeed different—the sixth Earl of Aberdeen. Years before, he had run away from the family estate. With his father's passing, he had become the new earl. Detectives were hired to take up his trail, following the torturous path from ship to ship, port to port. Always, they were one ship astern, one port too late.

Finally the dogged hunters located a Richmond, Va., pawnshop in which he had disposed of jewelry, a watch and a rifle. Each item was undisputably identified by the family crest. Closing the gap, the detectives continued on to his next stop, "a southern port," where they learned that he had shipped before the mast, bound for Australia on the schooner *Hera*.

Triumphantly, they booked passage aboard the fastest steamer bound for the lower continent, and when *Hera* waddled her weary way into Melbourne's outer harbor, the detectives met her by launch. Eagerly clambering aboard, they had asked for the seaman, George Osborne, to be told that he had been lost at sea during a storm. Upon examination of his effects, investigators found "abundant evidence that proved George Osborne and the Earl of Aberdeen were . . . one and the same." The long search for the missing heir was ended — and an ironic twist of history forgotten until years later, when ancient *Hera* went to her doom in the Graveyard of the Pacific.

Chapter 20

Death Stalked The Steamboating Jamiesons

From the wind-swept shores of Isle Arran they came, five brothers seeking their fortunes in the new land. But the steamboating Jamiesons, unlike most pioneers, were not to enjoy the fruits of courage and hard work. Instead, they were to meet sudden, violent death.

The story of the Jamieson brothers is one of the most intriguing tragedies in Northwest maritime history.

There were six brothers in the Jamieson family of Brodick. One became a clergyman and remained in Scotland, but Robert, Smith, Archibald and an unnamed brother chose to try their luck in the booming steamboat fleets of the Pacific Northwest. James, "baby" of the family, was left to complete his apprenticeship as machinist in a Firth of Clyde shipyard.

Smith and Archibald decided upon the white, rock-studded rapids of British Columbia's Fraser River, while Robert and the other brother joined the riverboat trade of Oregon. The sturdy Scotsmen soon made names for themselves throughout the Northwest for their reliability and skill as swiftwater pilots. Then, in 1854, tragedy struck for the first time when the unnamed brother's steamer, *Gazelle,* blew up at her dock in Oregon. Then there were four.

Three years later, the steamer *Portland* was carried over Willamette Falls. Among her dead was Robert Jamieson. Then there were three.

When several Yale businessmen formed the Yale Steam Navigation Company, they raised sufficient funds to build a steamer "second to no boat on the northern waters." Costing $23,000 — then a considerable sum for a riverboat — the *Fort Yale* was touted as being the finest craft braving the Fraser's treacherous rapids. During her first five months of service, under the able command of popular Captain Smith Jamieson, the new steamboat maintained a busy schedule between Yale and New Westminster.

On her last voyage, she had cleared the Royal City and headed upriver on schedule. It was just above Hope, at the murderous narrows known as Union Bar Riffle, that disaster found the Jamiesons for a third time, April 14, 1861.

Twenty-six-year-old Smith Jamieson was at the helm, 10 minutes before the accident, talking with passengers H. Lee Alley, Captain William Irving, of the river steamer *Colonel Moody,* and George Landvoigt. When the dinner bell rang, Captain Irving had offered to stand Jamieson's watch while he ate with the others.

To which Jamieson had laughed: "No, you don't! No opposition steamboat captain can steer this boat for me!" And with that, a grinning Irving had followed his fellow passengers to the saloon. Actually, Mr. Alley had lingered some moments as he was not hungry, before deciding to join the others.

They left Captain Jamieson in the wheelhouse with crewman James Allison — and but minutes to live.

The passengers had just begun dinner when, without the slightest warning, *Fort Yale* disintegrated in a horrendous blast as her boiler exploded.

"The noise," express agent Alley later described, "resembled, together with the crash, a heavy blow upon a sharp-sounding Chinese gong. The cabin floor raised and then fell in; at the same time the hurricane roof fell upon us, cutting our heads more or less, and blocking up all means of escape forward of the dinner table. We quickly made for the windows and doors in the after-part of the cabin, and got on the roof of the hurricane house, and there beheld a scene that baffles all description, and such as I trust I may never witness again.

"The boat, but a few seconds before nobly bucking against the swift current, was now a sinking mass of ruins from stem to stern — scarcely anything remaining in sight above water, but a small portion of her bow and the after-part of her saloon, and those gradually disappearing below water. Firewood, trunks, barrels, boxes, and thousands of splinters from the wreck were floating on the water," he continued. "Five or six human beings, their faces streaming with blood, and presenting an awful appearance, were struggling for life. Several jumped overboard, but on seeing the roof still afloat, desired to be hauled aboard again, and were got on by those of us on the roof — the port side of which was five inches out of water away aft, and the starboard side about level with the water. All the time we were floating downstream rapidly towards Hope."

Twenty minutes after the blast, the frightened, stunned and bleeding survivors still clinging to their swirling raft, several Indian canoes appeared, paddling desperately to overtake the wreck. Finally pulling alongside, the gallant natives took off most of the injured. Captain Irving, a Captain Grant of the Royal Engineers, Mr. Alley and several other volunteers remained with the hulk, intending to halt its frenzied flight downriver.

As the smoking ruin hurtled through the rapids, the men attempted to throw a line ashore in hopes of stopping her "if possible from going below Hope. But it was all in vain, for as soon as we got fast the line and the stern of the boat came to bear on it, (it) snapped like twine, although a large-sized hawser of 2½ inches in diameter. We tried twice or three times, and gave it up, and away she went down to the first bar below Hope, and there she lodged a total wreck."

Hope blacksmith Samuel Powers, fireman Joel Osborne (also known as James Growler), cook Joshua Buchanan and an unidentified deckhand had been killed instantly in the blast. James Allison, in the pilothouse with Jamieson, had been blown skyward, but, miraculously, fell back into the wreckage—suffering little more than a bruising. Engineer McGreavy, at his post in the engine room, was saved by the fact that the vessel's freight was situated between him and the boiler. Thomas King, deckhand, was not as fortunate, a leg having to be amputated below the knee. Several other crewmembers and passengers were slightly injured.

Of poor Smith Jamieson, there was not a trace—"a man standing on shore saw Captain Jamieson go up into the air among the splinters." The wreckage and both banks of the river for some miles were thoroughly searched without success, and it was feared he had been "blown to atoms."

Among those who mourned the missing mariner was the *Colonist:* "Although only a short time on the river, yet by his quiet, gentlemanly and honorable deportment, he has secured the good will of all and the warm esteem and friendship of many . . . As a navigator he was skilful, fearless and successful; as a captain, a universal favorite; and as a gentleman, unspotted."

"Poor Jamieson!" sighed friend Alley. "He was a quiet, unassuming man, of noble and generous impulses, and none who understood his nature as I did could but like him and mourns his untimely end."

Jamieson was to have been married that week.

Pieces of *Fort Yale's* ruptured boiler were found half a mile from the scene of disaster. Blacksmith Powers' body had been found on the shore, far from the wreck. The force of the explosion had stripped him of every piece of clothing.

Days later, search parties still hunted for Jamieson's body, deckhand King lay near death, Inspector of Steamers Westgarth opened an investigation into the tragedy, salvors stripped the wreck of cargo and machinery, and Osborne and Powers were buried at Hope. The *Yale's* helm, only slightly damaged, was recovered by Indians below Harrison River.

In Victoria, patrons of the Brown Jug Saloon viewed a twisted piece of the ill-fated steamer's boiler over their beer. Those who knew about such things solemnly pronounced the grim memento to be "composed of very inferior metal."

A reader wrote the *Colonist:* "Poor Jamieson was beloved by all 'poor travellers,' and long will his loss be felt by those who can appreciate the commendation — too rarely found — of careful skill and gentlemanly bearing."

Now there were but two riverboating Jamiesons.

The final, tragic act in the life of 35-year-old Archibald and "baby" James had begun months before, in the early summer of 1860, when the keel of a sidewheel steamer was laid in Victoria's Inner Harbor. Designed to run between the city, Harrison River and Hope, the building steamer was Captain Archibald's pride and joy: "The greatest care was bestowed upon her construction and one of the most experienced shipbuilders on the Pacific Coast came from San Francisco to superintend the work.

"As the vessel was fashioned into shape day by day her elegant lines won general admiration. She was meant to have speed and with this object in view engines and boiler of special design and great capacity and strength were ordered from Glasgow before the keel was laid here."

It had been intended that the *Cariboo,* as the new sidewheeler was christened, be ready that fall, but a series of mishaps delayed her completion by almost a year. Once, when finishing touches were being applied to her hull, timbers supporting her gave way, plunging the mammoth weight onto workers. One man died instantly, two were seriously injured; one of them maimed for life.

When the hull had been raised and reset in its cradle, work continued. Finally came the day of launching. But, instead of gliding down the ways as expected, the recalcitrant lady stuck fast. And there she remained until harried workers jacked her, inch by protesting inch, into the sea.

Then, as if all this had not been enough, Captain Jamieson encountered yet another delay when her engines did not arrive. In fact, they did not reach Victoria until the following spring when — finally — the machinery arrived. The same ship brought a second pleasant surprise for Jamieson, then in mourning for brother Smith: young James — "tall, stalwart...of about 24 years" — had completed his apprenticeship and was following in his brothers' footsteps.

It was arranged that William Allen, unemployed since his ship *Caledonia's* boiler exploded, would be hired as temporary engineer,

James to assume charge after a few voyages. In July, 1861, ill-starred *Cariboo* completed her maiden voyage to Harrison River, developing "great power and speed... The *Cariboo's* performances gave satisfaction to (Archibald)."

Midnight, August 2, 1861, *Cariboo* lay at her dock at the foot of Bastion Street, Victoria. Among the crowd of well-wishers bidding farewell to adventurers setting out for the Cariboo goldfields was early-day journalist David W. Higgins, there to see friend Count Paul de Garro and his faithful black retriever board the steamer.

Sailing time came and passed without the arrival of Captain Jamieson. Although steam was up, *Cariboo* ready to sail on schedule, Archibald was not to be seen. When he still failed to appear, Higgins decided he could wait no longer and walked to his quarters at the corner of Birdcage Walk and Belleville Street, beside the Inner Harbor. "I retired to bed," he recounted some 40 years after, "but for the life of me I could not sleep. A little clock on the mantel struck one and then half-past one o'clock and still I tossed from side to side. Sleep, although wooed with ardor, would not come to me. I was possessed with a strong feeling that an indefinable horrible something was about to occur.

"Every little while I could hear the *Cariboo* blowing off what seemed to be 'dry' steam in long-drawn volumes and disrupting the night air with the shrill notes of her whistle for miles around which must have disturbed others beside myself. At last I heard the 'cher-cher-cher' of the paddles and then I knew that the *Cariboo* was off."

At last, thought a relieved Higgins, he could sleep. As the sounds of the departing steamer grew fainter, he settled back, when—"a rending, tearing, splitting sound fell upon my ears. The 'cher-cher-cher' ceased instantly and the house shook as from the convulsive throb of an earthquake. The little timepiece on the mantel which had just chimed two trembled, reeled and stopped as if affrighted by the shock. In an instant I comprehended what had happened.

"The *Cariboo* had blown up!"

Alas, Higgins was all too correct. Just off what is now Fisherman's Wharf, *Cariboo* had been splintered by an awesome blast as her boiler erupted. Higgins hastily pulled on his clothing and ran for the Hook and Ladder Company's fire bell but was beaten by a young woman. With the bell arousing residents not awakened by the blast, Higgins ran for the waterfront, meeting a Scotchman named Wallace. The two men impressed a boat at the wharf and rowed for the scene of carnage.

"The dim light of approaching day enabled us to discern the late fateful craft lying a helpless, misshapen mass and drifting with the tide . . . A few lanterns were moving fitfully among the ruins. The upper deck had fallen in and the lower deck had been blown to pieces, but fortunately the bottom was unimpaired, and as the wreck did not sink it was towed into a little cove and anchored there for safekeeping. In the water at the side of the steamer we found the dead body of James Jamieson, the second engineer... Captain Jamieson had disappeared, nor was any trace of him found for many days when the sea gave up his mutilated form.

Fraser River pilot Henry Gray had been standing at Captain Jamieson's side when he stepped out of the pilothouse to adjust the binnacle lamp. The next Gray knew, he was standing on the main deck, uninjured, the hurricane deck in splinters about him. A passenger had been standing beside young James at the boiler, talking. "When the steam and smoke had cleared the passenger found himself near the spot where he stood when the explosion occurred while the engineer had been killed." Chief engineer Allen and mate John Sparks were found in the shattered debris; they had died instantly.

The body of Higgins' friend, Paul de Garro, was later found in the sea.

"Pieces of the boiler," Higgins recalled, "the iron of which was of unusual thickness, were picked up on the boat and a few fragments were found on the shore. What remained of the shell of the boiler was deposited on the beach near the tragic scene. I saw it lying there 35 years after the calamity. It was covered with barnacles..."

Engineer Allen was censured at the inquest for negligence, the coroner's jury ruling that "the cause of the explosion was too little water in the boiler. When the steam was blown off in vast volumes the boiler was emptied and when the water was turned on it fell on red hot plates with the natural result."

Like the helm of the *Fort Yale,* that of *Cariboo* was found in the water, undamaged. Archibald had had the wheel in his hands at the time of the blast; as had brother Smith when killed. Fate had been even unkinder to Archibald. But days before, he had turned down a handsome offer for his new ship. Long after the disaster, editor Higgins learned why Jamieson had been late in sailing on that fateful morning of August 2, 1861: He had "had a presentiment of evil and wished to remain in port till the next day."

Sadly, he had changed his mind and sailed, two and a-half hours later.

Victoria's last link with the ill-fated brothers was a headstone in Pioneer Square, long since removed. The inscription read:

"In memory of Smith Baird Jamieson, who lost his life by the explosion of the steamer *Yale* on the Fraser River, 14th April, 1861. Also Archibald Jamieson, and James Baird Jamieson, who are interred here, and who lost their lives by the explosion of the steamer *Cariboo* in Victoria Harbor, 2nd August, 1861. Three brothers, sons of the late Robert Jamieson, Brodick, Isle of Arran, Scotland."

And then there were none.

Chapter 21

The John Bright *Tragedy*

Storm, tide and reef: the cause of shipwreck along the exposed western shore of Vancouver Island is almost as varied as the names of its victims.

But for the courage and dogged persistence of one man, the tragedy — and mystery — of the barque *John Bright* might never have been solved.

The man who, more than a century ago, "walked with life in hand among ferocious Hesquiats" to uncover a terrifying tale of shipwreck and murder, was Captain James Christensen, sealer, trader, tugboat skipper and pilot. It was in his capacity as master of the little trading schooner *Surprise* that he uncovered the first hint of a tragedy which had begun with the sailing of the *John Bright* from Port Gamble, Wash., with a cargo of lumber for Valparaiso.

Master of the heavily-laden barque, Captain Burgess, was accompanied by his Chilean wife and family, consisting of three boys and two girls, and a 17-year-old maid. With her "golden hair and winsome face," the pretty English miss had caused quite a stir in the Puget Sound lumber port, where women were few and far between. Upon the *John Bright's* sailing, she had turned down no fewer than three proposals with the gay — and prophetic — announcement that she would never marry.

Finally loaded, the *John Bright* "hoisted her white wings and passed down the Straits to Cape Flattery," where adverse winds threw Captain Burgess off course. After days of battling the winter southerlies off Vancouver Island, the befuddled barque drove ashore near Boulder Point, Nootka Sound, within sight of the Hesquiat Indian village.

The *John Bright* had not been the only vessel to have been buffeted by the gale, Captain Christensen having sought shelter for his schooner in a cove some miles to the eastward. When the storm passed, he waited for the inevitable swarm of customers who, eager to trade, would paddle out to the schooner in their canoes. But hours passed without so much as a single customer and, bewildered, Christensen weighed anchor and cruised westward. Coming upon an old Indian fishing for salmon, the trader asked him why the villagers were not about. The fisherman replied that a ship was ashore at Hesquiat, and that there were three bodies on the beach.

At this, Captain Christensen immediately proceeded to Hesquiat. Upon approaching the village, he saw a large vessel on her beam ends, and completely awash in the breakers. Impatient as he was to land, the same seas prevented the *Surprise* from approaching too near and he had no choice but to again seek shelter. Thus, it was not until the following day that he was able to land at the Hesquiat camp. However, while waiting for the wind to die down, he had questioned several other natives, and had received contradictory accounts as to the nature of the wreck and the number of victims. One report indicated that there had been two casualties, one a woman, while another source insisted that there was but a single corpse.

By this time, Christensen was impatient to learn full details and, at first opportunity, sailed for the scene of the wreck, to drop anchor off the Hesquiat village, when several of the villagers paddled out to the schooner.

"What is this I hear about bodies on the beach, John?" he asked in Chinook of Anayitzaschist, the man commonly known to traders as John. But, to his surprise, John, who usually was more than willing to tell all the latest in tribal gossip, had no answer, merely shaking his head with a sullen frown. In growing suspicion and anger, the captain retorted: "Come now, John. All the way along the coast I have heard of bodies on the beach. At first it was three, then two, then one, and now you tell me none.

"Now, John," he continued grimly, "you were in the sawmill at Alberni long enough to know what to do in case of shipwreck. If I write down to Victoria, and report to them that bodies were washed ashore, and that you did not bury them, they will send a warship up after you."

Again he was amazed when his threat of a man-of-war not only failed to loosen John's tongue, but made him extremely angry. Lapsing into his native dialect, he swore vehemently, waved his arms in the air, then leaped over the railing and into his canoe. Although mystified by his response, the trader knew better than to push the point further and, concealing his concern, resolved to learn the reason for John's strange conduct for himself.

Quietly launching a canoe, he paddled for some distance along the beach without seeing anything out of the ordinary. But, near the wreck, and above the high-water mark, he came upon the remains of a woman. Although reduced to a skeleton, its sex was revealed by its long, flowing hair, which lay near the remains, although severed from the head. Nearby, he found further remains, which he judged to be those of a man. Both bodies had been stripped of clothing, although he could not immediately say whether this had been accomplished by surf or human hand.

After burying the bodies, Christensen paddled back to the *Surprise* and set sail for Victoria. On March 13, 1869, the little *Surprise* sailed into the Inner Harbor, to give the first word of tragedy; this, some five weeks after the *John Bright* crashed ashore at Hesquiat with the apparent loss of all on board. He immediately reported his discovery to Governor Frederick Seymour, although, as he told His Excellency, in his halting English, he was as yet unconvinced that the *John Bright's* lost company had met with foul play at the hands of the Hesquiats. But, as he emphasized to the governor, there were several features of the tragedy which did not add up, and he urged that a man-of-war be dispatched to the scene to investigate.

Seymour, however, was not convinced, and rejected Christensen's report with the argument that coastal traders were forever demanding the presence of a warship, with one pretext or another, for their protection. It was a charge that Seymour made more than once during his tenure as colonial governor; on this occasion, at least, it was not only inaccurate but ill-conceived.

Unable to gain satisfaction in Victoria, Christensen returned to Hesquiat two weeks later, determined to make a personal investigation of the wreck of the *John Bright,* although, as he well knew, he ran a great personal risk of offending the Hesquiats; particularly if, in fact, they did have something to hide.

On the northbound voyage, he stopped at neighboring Clayoquot, to pick up Ghwyer, the local chieftain. Together, the men landed upon the beach which Christensen had searched three weeks earlier. To the trader's horror, the sands, which had revealed no signs of tragedy during his first inspection, were now littered with human remains.

More than half a century after, puffing upon a large, evil-smelling cigar, the Danish mariner described that grisly scene: "First there was a leg here. Then an arm there. Then a trunk. There was not one solid body. And there were no heads. And they were all naked. It was a horrible spectacle.

"Scattered about the beach were the remains, in all, of nine men. The last body found was that of a large, well-built man, and was entire save for (the) head."

Gingerly approaching the corpse, Christensen and Ghwyer turned it over. Ghwyer was the first to notice the wound, his intent gaze drawing Christensen's attention to a gaping hole in the man's back. Upon recovering from his shock, the trader knew that his worst fears were realized. For there was no longer any question in his mind that the headless corpse on the sand had been murdered by a spear in the back.

With this grim conclusion came the realization that both he and Ghwyer were in danger. Burying the pathetic remains as hastily as they could, they retreated to the *Surprise* and sailed to Ucluelet where his employer, Captain William Spring, operated a trading post. Once there, he vented his anger at the outrage by writing a lengthy, and chiding, letter to Governor Seymour.

"Oh, but I was mad then," he recounted in 1924, having retired from the pilotage four years before, upon his 80th birthday. "The Governor had refused to send up a warship when I first told him of my suspicions. I was mad. After all the risk I had run, I thought the least they could have done was to send up a ship to investigate.

"But when the people at Victoria heard about it, they were so mad that they said if the Governor wouldn't send a ship up, they would equip a vessel and send her up themselves to find out just what had happened."

This time, however, Seymour was convinced as to the gravity of the situation at Hesquiat and did not require public outrage to move him to action. Shortly after Christensen's letter reached Victoria, HMS *Sparrowhawk* sailed for Hesquiat with a detachment of marines—and with Captain James Christensen aboard as pilot and interpreter. Upon arriving at the village, the investigators exhumed the bodies for examination, when seven of the villagers, including a chieftain named Katkinna, and John, the less than loquacious brave who had initially denied that any bodies existed, were taken into custody.

Tried in Victoria, the chief confessed to having been drunk when the ship drove ashore, saying that he had speared Captain Burgess in the back as the man tried to escape. John, he said, had murdered Mrs. Burgess when, caught in the surf, she had called to him for help. John had responded with outstretched hand, but, once upon the beach, said Katkinna, he had thrown her to the ground and shot her. According to testimony, only Mrs. Burgess and one seaman had been murdered the first day, the pretty English maid being dragged into the woods by a party of drunken braves. For hours, said a witness, her screams had "filled the air." Then there had been silence. When found, she had been decapitated. Although Christensen, and officers of the *Sparrowhawk,* made a determined search for her remains, the body was never recovered.

Much to Christensen's anguish, it was learned that, during his first visit to the Hesquiat village, Captain Burgess and his crewmen were yet alive, and hidden in the nearby woods under penalty of death if they attempted to attract his attention. When he had departed for Victoria, the villagers had waited several days to see if a warship came to investigate the wreck. When none appeared, they fell upon the crewmen. Minutes later, all were slaughtered, including the children.

But for Captain Christensen's suspicions, and determination, those who had sailed aboard the *John Bright* undoubtedly would have been given up as drowned in the surf. Upon conviction, Chief Katkinna and John were returned to Hesquiat and, upon the very spot where the survivors of the barque had dragged themselves ashore, hanged before their assembled tribesmen. As Captain Christensen put it, rather coldly, so long afterward, they "were roped up tight," and the scaffold left standing as a grim warning to all who would molest shipwrecked mariners.

Curiously, the trial and execution of Katkinna and John did not end the headaches caused by the case, officials in Victoria finding themselves stuck with a score of witnesses, many of them hostile, and including those who had originally been accused of having participated in the atrocity. Upon attempting to charter a trading schooner to take them home, they found that only the *Surprise* was available. This created an even greater problem, as Christensen could hardly be asked to take the Hesquiats aboard his vessel. As he had been the man responsible for uncovering the massacre, and the chief prosecution witness for the crown, there seemed little doubt that the Hesquiats would seek revenge.

Much to everyone's amazement, Christensen volunteered to take the natives home and, in due course, landed his passengers at Hesquiat. Although the tribesmen had outnumbered his crew, the voyage was completed without incident, the "resolute trader soon . . . back again in port with a whole skin and a very fine reputation for courage and seamanship . . ."

When, some 50-odd years after, he was asked why the Hesquiats had not killed him, Christensen replied: "That I don't know. I felt every minute I would be killed, but I wasn't afraid. I had got along well enough with them for seven years, and I thought I would take the risk."

But, in the Victoria home of his daughter, half a century and half a lifetime after the tragedy of the *John Bright,* he admitted: "Often now as I sit thinking at night and it comes back to me what it was like in those days, I wonder that I was allowed to live . . ."

Some time after the wreck of the *John Bright* was found, the barque's boom board was recovered. Inscribed in Latin was the legend, *Neminem Time—Neminem Laede:* Fear None—Injure None.

Chapter 22

Friday 13th Unlucky For Georgia *And The* Puritan

Friday, November 13, 1896, was indeed an unlucky one for Vancouver Island. For days, raging storms had bludgeoned the Northwest, causing widespread destruction—and death. Flooding Sooke rivers over-flowed their banks, washing away bridges and roads. Trying to ford one crazed stream, a Sooke resident was swept away. Two young Victoria men were drowned, a third rescued, when their tiny canoe capsized near Chatham Island.

Four days later, repairs were still under way. Battered ships, caught in Friday's gale—worst of the series—were limping into port. But two vessels did not make it.

Sadly, Victorians read of the loss of two familiar ships, an all-too-frequent occurrence in the perilous days when sail yet was common, and steam in its youth.

The 24-year-old tug *Georgia,* it was reported, "sank like a stone" in the treacherous waters of Queen Charlotte Sound. Retired as a government harbor craft, the venerable steamer had entered the cannery trade, towing log booms between regular assignments. Still believed to be "as staunch a craft of her class as any afloat," she was en route to Victoria for a thorough overhaul at the close of the canning season, when caught in the deadly gale.

For some reason, Captain Scott commanded her on this final voyage, although her regular master, Captain William Whitworth, was aboard. Also on board were his brother, Isaac Whitworth, as engineer, and a Victoria carpenter, George Blair.

In *Georgia's* wake danced a tiny clinker-built yawl, the masterpiece of an old Indian hunter. The native's superb craftsmanship was later praised by the four men, as, had it not been for the yawl, they never would have reached shore . . .

The weather was fair, with a freshening southeast breeze, when 20-ton *Georgia* cleared Rivers Inlet, January 11. By early afternoon, the wind was gale force and, caught in a flood tide between islands, *Georgia* was having a time of it. But the ancient tug was a fighter, her still-sturdy engines wheezing along at nine knots, her blunt bows spearing the waves.

Suddenly — "so suddenly that those aboard could hardly realize how it occurred" — a giant wave, roaring across the sea in a solid wall of water, smashed over the boat. *Georgia's* 75 feet reeled under the blow. Lurching drunkenly, she came to a stop. Her engine room had been flooded and her laboring propeller sighed to a final halt. Tackle and equipment had been swept from her decks by the wave, and now *Georgia* wallowed heavily, a naked, helpless hulk. The floating seas poured into her shattered hull.

Taking only time enough to grab their weather gear and some food, the crew abandoned ship. Casting off from her heaving stern, the little yawl pulled desperately away as, zig-zagging in a weird dance of death, *Georgia* slid under. In moments she was gone, her crew alone.

Then a blinding blizzard descended upon the four men wrestling against the sea in their yawl. For hours, they pulled on the slippery oars and baled, the cold biting hands and faces. Every moment brought fresh danger of their being capsized. Then two oars were yanked from benumbed fingers, and keeping the bow into the storm became doubly hazardous. One man sank to the bottom of the boat. "Chilled to the marrow and utterly disheartened," he had given up.

For 11 agonizing hours, Captain Whitworth and tortured companions fought the gale in their frail craft. But the "best little boat ever built" was made of strong stuff. Swept up on 40-foot waves, then thundering down into bottomless canyons, she struggled on.

Finally, she drove ashore on an isolated beach. There, her exhausted but ecstatic crew waited until the storm eased, then pulled for Wannuck, where they later boarded the steamer *Barbara Boscowitz* for Victoria, their original destination.

The 10-man crew of the San Francisco schooner *Puritan* had an equally miraculous escape.

The *Puritan's* ordeal began Thursday. For hours, the ship had been battered by the gale. But, after 30 years at sea, during which time he had never lost a ship, Captain C.H. Atwood was not worried. *Puritan* was only eight-years-old, handled well, and was a stout vessel. Bound in ballast for Port Gamble, Washington, by his reckoning she should be 68 miles southwest of Tatoosh Light; thereby leaving him ample room in which to manoeuvre.

Peering ahead into the darkness, Captain Atwood could see nothing, when, stiffening in surprise, he squinted into the night beyond the starboard bow. There it was again: a thin, wavering white line. Breakers!

Shouting the alarm to his helmsman, Atwood ran to the bow. With pounding heart, he realized that it was too late, that his ship was virtually surrounded by reefs. The heavy seas continued to drive his 614-ton schooner ever deeper into the rocks, and ripping out her bottom in the process.

In the matter of seconds, the proud *Puritan* was reduced to a splintered hulk. Perched high on the jagged reefs, the waves broke over her decks as Captain Atwood and crew lashed themselves to the rigging. Atwood had instantly decided that it would be suicidal to attempt reaching shore.

By morning, the frightened seamen had no choice but to remain aboard their disintegrating ship—the lifeboats had been smashed or swept away in the night.

With daylight, they could see shore was fully one-quarter of a mile away. The nearest of the rocks studding the seabed was 75 yards distant. The storm had calmed somewhat, but a heavy swell continued to pummel the *Puritan*. Marooned on the remains of their lumber schooner, the sailors could only wait and pray.

But Bonilla Point, where they had driven ashore, was a lonely spot that had claimed ships before the *Puritan*. Unless the nearby Carmanah Point lightkeeper spotted them, they would have a very long wait for help.

Rescue came in the guise of an Indian fisherman and his wife, who chanced upon the scene shortly after dawn. "With great difficulty," Frank Knighton "got safely through the breakers with his canoe," finally reaching the tiny islet nearest the *Puritan*. He was still too far away to throw or to catch a lifeline, but this did not daunt the heroic native.

It was low tide, and Knighton inched as far out into the surf as he could. There, the threshing waves up to his armpits, he unwound his fishing line, weighted it with a stone, and began casting towards the wreck. His intention was plain: he would try landing his line within reach of the sailors who, in turn, would drag the water with fishing lines. If they could hook his line, they would tie it to a hawser, which he would draw in and secure ashore. Thus, the seamen could scramble to land and safety.

But it was not to be that way. The distance was so great that most of his throws landed far too short. Then, if he did cast his line near the wreck, the taunting seas swept it back, or the stone weight dragged it under before the *Puritan's* men could snare it.

Time and again, he cast his line without success. Time and again, the surf swept him off his feet, dashing him against the razor-edged rocks. But the fisherman would scramble back to his lonely post. He was tired, bruised. His arms ached, exhaustion dragged at his body. Still he continued his lonely ordeal.

How many times he threw his line, how many times it sank or was carried out of reach of the *Puritan* by currents, how many times the sailors snagged bottom and had to replace their hooks, neither he nor they could guess. Aboard the wreck, the sailors took turns with the lines. But no one could relieve Knighton.

But he would not give up.

The seamen, driven almost mad by the worst anger of all, that of helpless frustration, gained strength and hope from their unknown friend. They needed it, for the *Puritan* was fast breaking up underfoot. Her cabins had been carried away, the hull was completely flooded. How many hours remained before she was pulled into deeper water, they did not dare guess.

Finally, hundreds of attempts later, the two fishing lines snaked towards each other, sank together in the creaming surf. Ever so cautiously, the seamen and the Indian drew in their strings.

For long seconds the slack was reeled in. Suddenly the lines broke water as one precious, dripping lifeline between ship and shore.

They had hooked!

The rest was relatively easy. A light rope was tied to the line and ship. The Indian hauled it in, when another, stronger hawser was secured to the first. Again, Knighton drew it to shore, and securely anchored it in the rocks. Saving nothing but the clothes on their backs, the seamen abandoned *Puritan's* swaying, groaning decks. Minutes later, all were safely on land.

After a brief rest, their attention was drawn to a grim memento of another unfortunate ship. Where they had landed were the gaunt bones of the American bark, *Lizzie Marshall*, which wrecked 12 years earlier. (Nearly two dozen ships have died here).

By this time, the neighboring lightkeeper had spotted the wreck, and arrived on the scene. Thomas Daykin offered food and what warm clothing he could. The American tug *Richard Holyoke* then chanced along, Daykin signalling her to pick up the shipwrecked mariners. But the tug sighted a customer and was off.

"It interested her more than we poor . . . chaps," Captain Atwood said bitterly. "There was money in a tow, so she left us and went after the ship."

After spending the night in their Indian savior's hut, and resting a day at Carmanah lighthouse, the refreshed seamen and Daykin made the 80-mile voyage to Victoria by oar. By then, *Puritan* was a total loss. Her four tall masts had collapsed, and the vessel lay broadside to the pounding seas. In days, she was gone.

For his role in this forgotten drama, fisherman Frank Knighton was awarded a medal. Ironically, news accounts of the time failed to give his name.

Chapter 23

A Phantom Pilot Saved The Eliza Anderson

A relic of the earliest days of steamboating on Puget Sound, they politely said of the ancient sidewheel steamer *Eliza Anderson*, in 1897. Old, tired and retired, she had been outfitted at the Moran shipyard in Seattle for one last fling, the carrying of a load of human freight to the Klondike.

After a quick overhaul—what couldn't be patched or painted over was ignored—the onetime famous lady was "ready" for the wilds of the northern coast. To say the least, the *Anderson* of 1897 was a far cry from the trim, respectable lady of 40 years before when, upon her arrival on Puget Sound in 1859, the 275-ton, 144-foot-long sidewheeler had enjoyed instant popularity on the Olympia-Victoria mail run. Also serving Steilacoom, Seattle, Port Townsend and way ports, the *Anderson*, a typical walking beam sidewheeler of the day, set no speed records. In fact, it has been said of her that no other vessel in Pacific Northwest history was slower than the *Eliza Anderson*—or made money faster.

For the *Anderson* was a trooper; steady and as reliable as a dollar watch. For almost 40 years, she served between Puget Sound and British Columbia ports. But, finally, a depressed economy, stiffened competition and old age conspired against her and she was at last tied up by her latest owners, the Northwestern Steamship Company. At her berth on the Duwamish River, the aging steamboat waited patiently for the inevitable voyage to a scrapyard.

As it turned out, fate held more in store for the faithful *Anderson* than an ignominious end at the hands of shipbreakers. Instead, three years later, the sidewheeler was to put to sea one last time...to sail on a voyage which would make West Coast maritime history—and baffle mariners for more than half a century.

Early in August, 1897, the *Anderson* sailed northward for St. Michael, Alaska, under the command of Captain Tom Powers, and in company of as strange a cavalcade of vessels as ever distressed an underwriter. The *Anderson* proceeded under her own steam, as did the tug *Richard Holyoke* (another Pacific Northwest pioneer, being one of the first deepsea propeller-driven tugs built on Puget Sound, some 20 years before), and the 108-foot sternwheeler *W.K. Merwin*. Under tow of the *Holyoke* was the old Russian gunboat, *Politofsky*, which was to serve this mis-matched flotilla as fuel barge, and the little schooner *William J. Bryant*, with its four passengers, as stores ship.

Crowded aboard the *Anderson* was a motley collection of adventurers and characters, ranging from the notable to the notorious, tin-horn gamblers rubbing shoulders with the respectable and the religious. Harmony between passengers and crew, it seems, was lacking in the extreme, arguments and worse being the order of the day as this seagoing circus limped northward through the Inside Passage between Vancouver Island and the British Columbia mainland. Making Captain Powers' task of keeping the *Anderson* afloat and on course all the more difficult was the fact that the steamer's list of appointments did not include such luxuries as a compass. Further problems arose at Comox, V.I., when the old steamer collided with the sailing ship *Glory of the Seas*; fortunately for that vessel, confining most of the damage to her own starboard paddle box.

Somehow, the *Anderson, Holyoke, Politofsky, Merwin* and *Bryant* lumbered on, defying the elements and all commonsense as they slowly made their way northward. However, once off Kodiak Island, matters became increasingly serious as a storm ravaged the fleet, finally snapping the *Merwin's* towline. Amazingly, the good tug *Holyoke* managed to restore this vital hawser, although not without considerable difficulty. Then the *Anderson* did her part to enliven the occasion by running out of coal—precisely at the peak of the storm.

From the start, those who had paid for their passage aboard the *Anderson* had known discomfort and dissatisfaction. Tempers had flared from the moment the eager fortune hunters piled aboard and charged to their reserved cabins and berths—only to find that the ship's owners, who knew a gold mine without ever having set foot in the fabled Klondike—had sold the staterooms and bunks two, and often three, times. Under the circumstances, it had been a matter of first come, first served—or whoever was the toughest—in settling accommodation. For those who arrived late, or were unwilling to resolve the matter by duel, fisticuffs or cards, and unable to find room in the ship's saloon, it was the hard, open deck—and a long, unpleasant voyage to Alaska.

Things became decidedly more unhappy when, caught in the gale north of Prince Rupert, the weary *Anderson* began to toss and turn crazily, as Captain Powers and crew fought to keep her head into the wind. This navigational necessity was made all the more difficult when her chief engineer reported the steamer to be out of coal and, unable to refuel her bunkers from the *Politofsky* as originally planned, Captain Powers had no choice but to order his men and passengers to ravage the vessel for firewood. In the next few hours, every piece of flammable furniture and fitting that could be spared was chopped up and sacrificed to the great god, steam. Many of those of the sidewheeler's company not so employed, turned to even more pressing matters, such as prayer, the Rev. Mr. Clark of New Hampshire saving a growing number of souls as the hours advanced—and as the *Anderson*'s chances of surviving the storm seemed to diminish.

As proof of their reclamation, several of the ship's gambling fraternity ditched cards and dice. For his part, Captain Powers made sacrifices of his own, instructing the crew to pour almost 50 barrels of lubricating oil and kerosene over the bow in an attempt to calm the waves.

Almost as great a threat to the *Anderson*'s terrified company as the gale, was the condition of the steamer herself. For the twice-retired side-wheeler had been neglected for far too long. During her first mothballing, years before, she had been abandoned, half-submerged, in a muddy slough, much of her original equipment being stripped by scavengers as knee-high weeds grew on her decks. Partially restored, she had re-entered service before again being laid up and, ultimately, refitted for the run to Alaska. But repairs had been purely makeshift— anything to shave costs—and how she passed steamboat inspection, even in that carefree age, defies reason. Likely, some of the money which should have been spent on repairs had been used to ease her through inspection.

Grim proof of the *Anderson*'s condition came when her tall smokestack crashed to the deck, creating even greater headaches for a beseiged Captain Powers and his officers. Interestingly enough, however, the steamer's crew (quite likely a woe-begotten assortment of waterfront derelicts and inexperienced adventurers working their way to the gold fields) seems to have performed reasonably well under the circumstances. The fact that their lives depended upon their keeping the *Anderson* afloat and underway undoubtedly inspired all, passengers included, to duty. All were kept busy, the seamen working to set out a sea anchor, repair the rudder chains (so rusted that they broke not once, but several times), clean the steam pumps, which continually clogged with coal dust from the flooded bunkers, and pour oil on the charging waves from the bow. Passengers did their bit by taking turns at the pumps as firemen continued to axe furniture and cargo for fuel.

For two days and two nights, the exhausted *Anderson* struggled against the storm, kept afloat by a fervent combination of patchwork and prayer. By this time, as it became more apparent that the sidewheeler must ultimately yield before the onslaught of wind and wave, the energetic Mr. Clark was able to take grim satisfaction in the fact that his work of spreading the Word throughout the ship had been almost universally successful. The most backward of sinners among her company had seen the light and willingly forsaken evil ways; the conversions likely prompted by the fact that the *Anderson* was rapidly running out of fuel once more, the firemen having been forced to the extreme of draining the steamer's wooden water tanks and chopping them up for fuel, the cook having contributed the last side of bacon from the galley.

By the third morning, the end was approaching for the *Eliza Anderson*. Not only was she almost out of fuel, and fast taking on water, but heroic Captain Powers had lost all track of his position. For all he knew, the sidewheeler could be on a collision course with some submerged rock...he just did not know.

Exactly what happened at this point is a matter of some dispute, today, more than three-quarters of a century after. According to one account, the *Anderson's* salvation came in the form of a small sailboat which, defying the rollicking seas, steadily overtook the laboring steamer. Upon coming alongside, the craft's lone occupant, "a veritable giant of a man, rawboned and muscular," clambered over the side and onto the *Anderson's* deck, to make his way, without a word, to the pilothouse, where an exhausted and anxious Captain Powers and officers were yet at their posts. With his long grey hair and beard, and looking as though he had stepped from the pages of the Old Testament, the stranger took a position beside the helmsman. Then, throughout that memorable night, he gave terse instructions as he felt necessary.

Unerringly, he guided the *Anderson* past reef and islet until, at long last, the storm was almost spent and the steamer safely anchored in the snug of a tiny island cove. When the *Anderson* was secured alongside the dock of an abandoned cannery, the silent stranger climbed into his boat and sailed away without a word of explanation as to his identity or as to how he had come to spot the steamer's predicament.

According to this source, the identity of the "phantom pilot" was never learned. His appearance at the height of the storm, and his sudden departure when the ship was safe, assumed, over the years, an uncanny quality which made more than one of the *Anderson's* passengers and crew wonder if they had not imagined the entire incident.

Whatever, the *Eliza Anderson* and company were safe and, having refuelled from the old cannery's coal pile, they limped on to Unalaska,

144

where the passengers showed their feelings for the *Anderson* by immediately abandoning her; continuing on to the mouth of the Yukon by sealing schooner. And there, far from her home waters of Puget Sound, *Eliza Anderson* awaited her fate for the third and final time. This time, there was no reprieve and, a year after her miraculous arrival, a storm parted her mooring lines and she drove ashore. Before long, she had been reduced to little more than a memory, her bones scattered on the beach.

As for the other illustrious vessels which had accompanied her during that epic northern voyage, only two, the tug *Holyoke* and the schooner *Bryant,* lived to see Washington waters again. After two seasons on the Yukon River, the *Merwin* was taken to Nome, where she went ashore and was gradually pounded apart. The old *Politofsky,* returned to her home waters of Russian America, also died at Nome.

But if the *Eliza Anderson* was gone, the mysterious circumstances surrounding her "phantom pilot" and providential escape from certain destruction continued to haunt students of marine lore for years afterward. Another version of that incredible last voyage is to the effect that the stranger had not overtaken the *Anderson* by small boat, but had suddenly appeared at Captain Powers' side in the steamer's pilothouse, to guide her through a maze of breakers and reefs to a safe harbor. Described as having a beard, the eerie stranger seems to have vanished immediately upon the steamer's making a safe anchorage, not being seen again by any of those aboard the ship. This spooky coming and going convinced some that the mysterious pilot was not of the same worldly plane.

Two years after, a Seattle newspaper published an account in which an "old sailor" who had been aboard the *Anderson* identified the pilot as the ghost of Captain Tom Wright, onetime owner and master of the sidewheeler during her heyday on Puget Sound. "Captain Tom's spirit," explained the seaman, "saw our danger. He knew and loved the *Anderson,* and that was how it happened that a stranger came out of the storm and brought us safely to land."

There were those, of course, who had other, more practical, explanations for the phenomenon. Twenty-odd years ago, another of those who had sailed aboard the *Anderson* wrote a magazine article about that amazing voyage. Fifty-six years after the steamer's escape, he wrote, he had met a former crewmember of the American revenue cutter *Corwin.* The cutter, this man told him, had been sent to search for the *Anderson* when her consorts, which safely reached port, reported her to have been lost in the storm.

In the course of the *Corwin's* search, the crewmen had questioned two brothers at Kodiak Island. Operators of a small cannery which had failed, the Scandinavians told him how one of the brothers, upon seeing the *Anderson* at Kodiak, as she prepared to sail for Unalaska, had boarded her as a stowaway, intending to see a relative at Un-alaska for a loan. Even when the steamer had been beset by storm and lack of fuel, he had remained hidden, sure that she would weather through the gale, and afraid that if he revealed himself he would be held for the authorities upon landing. However, when it became painfully evident that the sidewheeler must founder, he had introduced himself to Captain Powers and guided that officer to a safe anchorage near the cannery. Once the *Anderson* was secure, his brother had taken him off the *Anderson* by rowboat, both hiding in their isolated cabin until the vessel sailed. This Scandinavian cannery operator—at least, according to this version—was the "phantom pilot" who so mysteriously appeared at the height of the storm and guided the *Anderson* to safety.

Whichever he was—stowaway or ghost—the mystery pilot undoubtedly saved the *Eliza Anderson* and her exhausted company from certain destruction. And with that, the remarkable story of a remarkable ship was history.

Chapter 24

Shipwrecked Seamen Saved From Jaws Of Death

There was no hint of approaching disaster as night fell along Vancouver Island's west coast, January 22, 1909. Forty-two days out of Callao, bound in ballast for Port Townsend, the four-masted schooner *Soquel* ran before a gale. His seven-year-old, 767-ton coaster pitched heavily in the blizzard, but Captain Charles Henningsen was not worried. He had survived worse storms in his career; such as the time his barkentine the *Uncle John* pounded to pieces off Clo-oose when her anchors dragged.

But all that was past... This was his last voyage. His wife and infant daughter were sleeping peacefully below; when *Soquel* docked, Henningsen would return with his family to their California home. After so many years of long separations, they would be forever together.

It was midnight when the *Soquel* struck. Without warning, the lurching schooner slammed into a reef. In the terrifying seconds that followed, as his ship drove deeper into the rocks, Captain Henningsen realized the fatal truth: in the raging darkness, he had strayed too far north, mistaking the beacon at Pachena Point for Cape Flattery's Tatoosh Light. His schooner had been impaled on the Seabird Rocks in the Pacific Graveyard.

At the crash, according to the record, Henningsen "ran below and told his loved ones to remain there until he ascertained the extent of the damage. Too nervous to content herself below, Mrs. Henningsen wrapped a blanket about her three-year-old girl and came on deck, where Captain Henningsen at once cleared away a lifeboat and assisted her into it."

The *Colonist* described the horror that followed.

147

Henningsen "took the child and held it in his arms, while the pounding of the seas and the whistling of the wind through the cordage accompanied by sharp reports as the sails snapped drowned the voices of those who shouted all manner of commands as they ran about the decks. Then the mizzen and jigger masts snapped and came down with a crash. The big spar fell on...the little girl, knocking her from her father's arms, while he was knocked to the deck with a badly bruised back.

"As he scrambled to his feet he saw the end of the big spar fall across the lifeboat, striking his wife. He ran to her, just in time to see her expire. She had (had) a premonition of death. When she was lifted into the lifeboat she shrank back as a big comber broke against the schooner's side. The comber conveyed a sense of impending doom to her, and she exclaimed:

" 'This is death; kiss me, Carl.'

"He did. A moment later the spar came down as the wreck careened, wrecking the lifeboat, and killing both mother and child..."

Timbers breaking, decks awash in the thundering breakers, *Soquel* was in her death throes. As terrified seamen clambered into the rigging, the grief-stricken captain wandered the buckling decks, "wringing his hands, groaning, seemingly hardly conscious..."

First mate C.E. Svenson made himself heard above the roar, ordering five crewmen to help him lower the captain's gig. Strengthened by desperation, they heaved the tiny craft from the *Soquel's* side and frantically rowed for the solid wall of foaming white that was the beach. Their fragile gig did not have a chance. Within seconds, it was flooded, the end near. Then — miraculously — land! The sinking craft had scraped across a rocky ledge, midway between ship and shore. Svenson and comrades scrambled onto the reef, drenched and battered. But they were alive.

Aboard ship, the situation was worsening by the minute. Several of the remaining crew were for taking their chances in the last lifeboat, but Captain Henningsen, somewhat recovered, dissuaded them, aware that such a move would be suicidal in that mad sea. Two refused to listen, pleading with their fellows for help in lowering the boat.

"She's going any moment!" cried John Herman. "I'm not going to drown like a rat when I can make a fight of it! Who's with us?"

When none offered to join the daring duo, they shimmied along the spinnaker, hoping to leap to the rocks below. A towering wave hammered the schooner, snapping the boom like a match stick and plunging the seamen, screaming, to the deck. Herman writhed in agony, his leg broken.

Meanwhile, on the reef, mate Svenson struggled to light a fire. It was snowing again, and the hours passed slowly. At last, a ragged grey line in the east announced dawn. Its arrival brought little relief to the castaways, the gale screaming to greater intensity...

Although they could not possibly have known that help was at that very moment on its way, Pachena lightkeeper Irwin, who had spotted the wreck from his tower, had telephoned Bamfield, Captain W.H. Gillen and hardy lifeboat crew answering the call. Their sturdy new motorboat had itself been wrecked days before, forcing them to use the old lifeboat—powered by muscle. Fortunately, the Victoria steamer *Leebro,* on charter to the marine department, had put into Bamfield to pick up the motorboat and, upon embarking Gillen's crew, Captain James Hunter thrust his ship's blunt bow into the blizzard. Manoeuvring his bucking command as close in to the *Soquel* as he dared, Hunter held her in position by sheer nerve. And luck. Now it was up to Captain Gillen's crew.

Shoving away from the *Leebro's* side, the men matched courage and oars against the Pacific. To their 18-foot boat, each wave was a mountain; a mountain that descended upon them again and again with all the speed, sound and fury of a runaway locomotive. Their boat could not long stand such a battering and, halfway to Svenson's marooned party, Gillen reluctantly had to order about.

At 2 o'clock that afternoon—the *Leebro* had been vainly battling for more than five hours—the CPR steamer *Tees* arrived upon the scene on her regular run upcoast. Captain Gillam was a welcome arrival, his ships specially-built surf boats had clutched drowning sailors from raging seas before. Maybe they could accomplish the impossible again.

By this time, Gillen had launched *Leebro's* second boat and, securing a line to the *Tees'* boat, he drifted downwind toward the castaways' ledge. The threshing surf, however, was too much and, with a sudden lurch, the lifeboat spun onto its side, spilling the crew into the surf. Fortunately, all were able to grip the reeling boat and were hauled alongside the *Tees* by lifeline. Then, bailed out, the heroic crew tried again.

This time, they made it, hauling aboard the marooned seamen; that is, all but Svenson, the courageous mate refusing to be saved until those aboard the *Soquel* had been rescued. Captain Gillen tried to argue him into the boat, saying that there was not a chance of boarding the schooner in that sea; that they would have to wait. Svenson refused to move and, provided with some rations, he began a lonely vigil on the reef...

Aboard the *Soquel,* it was a nightmare. Seaman Herman huddled in the scuppers, moaning. Others shivered by a gunwhale, Captain Henningsen was yet "prostrated" with grief. The six had watched their comrades' rescue, then stared, horrified, as the lifeboats had struggled back to the ships. At nightfall, the *Lebro* and *Tees* headed for Bamfield until morning. They were alone.

Then a new visitor arrived. Fortunately, the U.S. revenue cutter

149

Manning was equipped with searchlights. Upon anchoring nearby, she played her powerful beam onto the wreck. It was little enough comfort to those aboard the *Soquel,* but they were grateful for small mercies, encouraged by the fact that they were not alone after all.

On the reef, mate Svenson huddled in his oilskins beside a driftwood fire, trying to sleep.

Sunday came at last. With a dawn came a low tide and a slackening wind, and *Soquel's* men saw their chance. If rescuers could not come to them, perhaps they could meet the lifeboats midway. Half carrying, half dragging injured Herman through the surf, they fought their way to Svenson's side.

"They waited confidently," reported the *Colonist,* "feeling that rescue was certain when the lifesavers returned. Not far away the wreck, with the mizzen and jigger gone, the standing yards away, lay listed over with spray breaking over as the seas pounded the impaled craft. Nearer the two boats lifted and fell in the long-lipped waves, standing in as close as possible, while one by one the eager lifesavers hauled the worn-out seamen...from the rock. One moaned with pain of his broken leg, another lay helpless in the bottom of the boat with a badly bruised back; all were worn to exhaustion."

That afternoon, the drama was ended. The battered Americans were taken aboard the *Manning* and on to Port Townsend.

Captain Gillen telegraphed a cryptic report to Victoria: "Crew all saved from wreck. *Leebro* transferring crew on board *Manning.* Will then go for Clo-oose lifeboat. Two dead bodies still on board wreck. I expect to recover these tomorrow morning at low water. *Tees* rendered valuable assistance. Sea fairly smooth now."

It had all been "a part of the day's work" for the lifeboat crew.

But if it had been routine to them, it certainly had not been routine to the *Soquel's* crew, a grateful Captain Henningsen later writing Captain Gillen from Port Townsend. Dated January 29, 1909, the letter ends: "...I beg to thank you, also your brave crew, for your noble, brave and ceaseless efforts in assisting in the rescue of myself and crew and shall write you fully after my arrival at San Francisco, and after I have been able to somewhat recover from my sad affliction.

"I am leaving here for San Francisco with the bodies of my wife and child on the steamer *Watson* tomorrow and will be pleased to have you notify Messrs. Rothschild and Company, my agents and representatives at Port Townsend by wire when you reach Victoria with the effects. They will telegraph you how to send the same over to them so that they can be forwarded to me.

"Again thanking you all for what you have done for me, more fully of which I shall write you from S.F., I am.,

Gratefully yours,
C. Henningsen."

Until his tragic death in 1930, Captain William Hugh Gillen was a very busy seaman. Born at Wine Harbor, Sonora, N.S., on the family farm in 1872, Gillen joined the famous Maritime fishing fleet at the age of 14. Six years later, he "went deep water," sailing out of Halifax for the West Indies and South America. An old discharge identifies him as an able seaman aboard the *Beta,* of Glasgow. He continued in this trade until 1895, when he came to the Pacific Coast.

After a hitch aboard the sealing schooner *Carrie C.W.,* he joined the 161-ton Victoria-based *Thistle.* There followed a terrifying voyage aboard the Shanghai barque *Nanaimo,* bound to Tientsin with lumber. According to his son, I.J. Gillen of Tsawwassen, B.C., "Gales off the China coast delayed her so long that provisions gave out. Freezing temperatures coated ship and deckload with ice; two of (the) Chinese crew died as a result of exposure, and 'everyone was minus a hand or foot or both.' The deckload eventually carried away, and the ship made Shanghai."

After six weeks in hospital, the mariner was again on duty. In following years Gillen tried his hand as quartermaster aboard the CPR's *Empress of China,* more sealing, tugboating in New York, as coxswain of the Bamfield lifeboat, before returning to towboating as mate of the *Chemainus.* Changing yet again, to fishing this time, he served as second mate aboard the *Celestial Empire,* then as mate of the *Flamingo.* The last discharge in possession of son Iver is from the five-masted schooner *Laura Whalen,* following a nine-month voyage to Australia. After several years of jobbing along the B.C. coast, Captain Gillen tasted the Arctic. One of his northern cruises was to Herschel Island to deliver the RCMP vessel *St. Roch.* A year later, he commanded the Hudson's Bay Company supply ship *Old Maid No. 2.* He was preparing her for a second voyage to Herschel in 1930, when "he mysteriously disappeared. His body was found about a month later. Cause of death: drowning."

A tragic end to a fine mariner; a man who thought it "part of the day's work" to snatch shipwrecked seamen from the clutches of death.

Chapter 25

Terror On The Ice

Victoria was in the headlines, in the spring of 1913, and residents were making the most of their new-found fame. A holiday spirit prevailed throughout the city, as citizens basked in the spotlight of the entire continent and Europe. For Victoria was about to launch one of the greatest scientific projects of the time.

A project that set out to the rousing strains of military bands and cheering crowds — and ended in shipwreck in the frozen Arctic wastes.

For this was the famous Canadian Arctic Expedition which has gone down in history as one of the worst northern disasters since the ill-fated Sir John Franklin trek into oblivion, more than 65 years earlier.

The brainchild of Manitoba-born Vilhjalmur Stefansson, the project had been months in the making. Previously, the 34-year-old explorer had made news on his first Arctic expedition for his discovery of "blond" Eskimos. He had determined that Victoria Islanders possessed "decided 'European' characteristics." He had offered three possibilities for such a phenomenon, saying that which he thought *least* probable was that these people were descendants of legendary Viking explorers.

This was excellent copy, and newspapers gave glowing details; headlines announced Stefansson's discovery of Eric the Red's descendants, crediting them with blond hair and blue eyes. Fifty years later, "Stef" would be recognized as one of the greatest Arctic explorers of the age. But, to his dying day, he was haunted by the then legendary accounts of his blond Eskimos. The real tragedy was the fact that some experts, upon reading the outrageous accounts which had become a Frankenstein to Stefansson, assumed him to be a sensationalist and a charlatan. This hurt him deeply, although, on the other hand, his schemes, lectures and books gained world-wide popularity with the general public due to his initial notoriety.

Immediately upon returning from the Arctic, he had begun planning his second expedition. His ambition was to do nothing less than chart the unknown Beaufort Sea and prove that there is abundant marine and animal life in the Polar Sea; not even Eskimos believing the latter.

With the help of Admiral R.E. Peary, conqueror of the North Pole, he convinced the National Geographic Society and the American Museum of Natural History of the need of such a project. After some negotiating, these august bodies and the Harvard Traveler's Club pledged $50,000 to outfit a ship.

Stefansson would direct the northern section, charged with exploring Beaufort Sea. Dr. R.M. Anderson, partner of the first four-year trip in the north, would head the southern section, carrying out general scientific observations.

Stefansson chose Arctic veteran Captain Theodore Pedersen as ship's master and told him to find a vessel. Pedersen decided upon the whaler *Karluk,* which entered Esquimalt, B.C., drydock for complete refitting.

By this time, Stef's plans were gaining steam — and his money fast disappearing. Hurrying to Canada, he tried to talk influential friends into subscribing to the project. They were interested, but poor. They did, however, arrange an interview with Prime Minister R.W. Borden. Consequently, the Canadian government agreed to underwrite all expenses if the original backers withdrew. The American institutions gracefully did so and, on February 22, 1913, an order-in-council made Vilhjalmur Stefansson and his men Canadian civil servants.

Months later, all was ready. In the final weeks of preparation, Victoria, headquarters during the expedition's preparation, was feverish with excitement. The day before *Karluk* sailed, a deputation of civic officials, the mayor and four aldermen boarded the little ship and presented four Canadian flags to Stefansson. The ensigns were to be raised over "any land that comes within the British empire as the result of discoveries made by the present expedition."

Said the *Colonist:* "Mayor Morley, in humorous vein, informed the explorer that the City of Victoria was always willing to extend her boundaries, and although it was not implied that the newly discovered land should be cut up in 50-foot lots and disposed of at the existing realty prices, the city which gave birth to such a magnificent expedition would not be averse to having new territory brought into line, if only by name."

Karluk herself was "loaded down with stores and equipment sufficient to tide the expedition over a period of two years. A ship never sailed from Victoria that carried a more varied cargo. In addition to the heterogeneous mass of nutrative foods and miscellaneous equipment necessary for an expedition of this character, there is stowed on the deck of the *Karluk* huge piles of overflow supplies... There was every conceivable thing from a pin to an anchor included in the 200 tons of supplies that have been hustled aboard...within the past few days. In addition to 150 tons of coal stowed away below decks, the vessel early this morning completed taking aboard an additional 50 tons of fuel on deck, which will be consumed during the passage of the vessel from Victoria to Nome."

The morning daily's attention to the ship's stores did not extend to her condition. Perhaps the reporter thought it tactful not to mention that the 250-ton square-rigged auxiliary vessel reeked of whale oil and was filthy. In the words of one of her party upon first boarding, "The quarters were like nothing I had ever seen—unpainted, crowded, smelly and swarming with cockroaches." Such was the ship Stefansson had to navigate the treacherous, ice-choked Arctic seas. In fact, if all went well, it was hoped to take her through the Northwest Passage.

Only one incident had marred the budding project to date: Captain Pedersen had resigned. Stefansson accepted his notice reluctantly, a man of such skill and experience being hard to find, and even harder to replace. However, Admiral Peary again came to his aid, suggesting Captain Robert Abram Bartlett, Peary's own ship-master. The Newfoundlander's reputation was unequalled and he was hired on the spot.

Thus Victoria found herself playing hostess to celebrities. Both Stefansson and Bartlett were famous, also Dr. Anderson. Even the premier and lieutenant-governor were in town to see *Karluk* off.

Dignitaries by the dozen attended a special luncheon in the Empress Hotel honoring the three notables. "...After the toast to the King," it was reported, "Sir Richard (McBride) arose and spoke briefly in well chosen words. He referred to the fact that the expedition is the largest one of a purely scientific nature that has ever visited the North. Mr. Stefansson, he said, is among the first of explorers, and Sir Richard mentioned the very great importance of the task about to be undertaken, which is to make known to the world, if possible, what there is in the last million square miles of the earth's surface awaiting exploration.

"He expressed great satisfaction because of the association of Dr. Anderson and Captain Bartlett with the work, drawing attention to the fact that it was through the latter's seamanship that Peary was able to sail within 400 miles of the Pole. He then presented Mr. Stefansson with a piece of plate, in commemoration of the departure of the expedition."

A "visibly affected" Stef accepted the gift, thanking all present, and paying homage to a "broad-minded" Canadian government. The silver platter was inscribed: "Presented by the Executive Council on

154

behalf of the people of the Province of British Columbia to Vilhjalmur Stefansson, head of the Canadian Arctic Expedition, on the occasion of the departure of the steamship *Karluk* from Victoria, B.C., for the Arctic Ocean, June 17, 1913."

The names of all party members would be engraved on the tray.

Thousands watched as tiny *Karluk,* loaded to the railings with supplies and coal, slipped from Esquimalt on her historic — and last — voyage. On a warm afternoon, flags waving, she signalled farewell to her adopted home. No one aboard or ashore could have known that the future held tragedy and death for many...

(There was something else that most, including Stefansson, did not know; that there already was trouble in the ranks. In the vast, frozen Arctic, where each man's life relied upon his neighbor, this discord would bloom with deadly results).

Nome was as excited as Victoria had been. Here, the expedition had already purchased the schooner *Alaska.* Now, Stefansson ransacked the town of every piece of equipment, sledges, Eskimo clothing, stores and dogs to be found. After his colossal buying spree, he discovered that his two little ships could not carry it all, so he bought the 30-ton auxiliary schooner *Mary Sachs.* Then, all details attended to, the small flotilla set sail to keep a date with disaster.

At Teller, they had to make an unplanned stop, the *Karluk's* boilers needing to be cleaned, the *Alaska* requiring repairs. When *Karluk* was ready, she and the *Mary Sachs* went ahead, leaving the *Alaska* to catch up when ship-shape. At sea, a sudden gale separated the two, tiny *Mary Sachs* keeping inshore, *Karluk* heading for deeper water. This was a taste of the coming tragedy: Bartlett was a good salt-water skipper, a veteran of the Atlantic and the Eastern Arctic. But he did not realize that Alaskan weather and tidal conditions operate quite differently to their eastern cousins.

Karluk encountered her first ice shortly afterward. Unless they rounded Point Barrow soon, they would have to wait as much as a full season for a second try. By the time the stout whaler had muscled her way to within 30 miles of the point, she was completely iced in. Drifting with the pack, she rounded Barrow. Then, breaking free, she steamed on to Cross Island, where she was totally blocked by pack ice.

It was here that Bartlett and Stefansson made the fatal error.

Aware of the fickle winds and currents, Stefansson instructed Bartlett to wait for an east wind to clear a channel along shore. He then retired. When he awoke, *Karluk* was underway. Bartlett had sought deep water, the only course to a seaman of his training. But Stefansson must share any blame to be attached to the approaching tragedy. For, as he admitted in his diary, he realized that Bartlett was wrong, that it was his, Stefansson's, duty to order the *Karluk* inshore. Instead, he agreed to wait and see what morning brought.

Dawn brought the worst—the *Karluk* was trapped. The ice held her fast in its steely grip. She would never escape.

August 17, 1913—exactly two months after she gaily cleared Esquimalt—a storm blew her back several miles. It was the beginning of the end. For a month, *Karluk* and her icy prison drifted westward, until off Harrison Bay. Here, Stefansson's optimism—nothing could hold him down for long—returned. It was possible that the *Karluk* would sit tight for the winter and be released in the spring thaw. As the ship was in need of fresh meat, he decided to hunt caribou. He chose anthropologist Diamond Jenness, secretary Burt McConnell, and the expedition's young photographer, George Hubert Wilkins, to accompany him. Wilkins would prove to be the perfect protege and, years later, Stefansson and a fascinated world would avidly follow the Australian's exploits and see him knighted.

Planning to return to the ship within two weeks, Stefansson took the two poorest sledges, saving the better ones for serious work later; also the poorest dogs. With just enough provisions to tide them over, the little safari set out. It was to be a long hunt...

Their first night "ashore," they camped on the ice. The next day, they made it to a small island, midway between ship and shore. As a savage September gale began sweeping the bay, they made camp and wrestled with pieces of driftwood, trying to construct a crude observation tower. Despite the icy wind, they succeeded, and took turns, between snow squalls, at seeing how the *Karluk* was weathering the storm.

Suddenly, the lookout squinted, unable to believe his eyes. The others incredulously confirmed his observation: *Karluk* was moving—against the wind. Had the gale dislodged her and Bartlett have her underway once more?

They slept fitfully, excited at this new turn of events. For two days and nights, the wind raged. When, at last, they could scan the white landscape, they could see no *Karluk*. She had vanished!

With her were "25 human beings, the best dogs, the best sledges, stores of food and clothing, rifles, ammunition, Wilkins' motion-picture equipment and scientific instruments that were invaluable and could not be replaced in the Arctic."

The storm had smashed the icefield, Stefansson's party finding itself marooned on a drifting ice floe just large enough to hold them and the dogs. A heavy swell jerked their tiny "raft" this way and that, threatening to pitch them into the frigid sea at every moment. Each collision with another floe seemed like an earthquake to the frightened company. With the *Karluk* gone, Stefansson, his three inexperienced companions, the dogs—with little food for men or beast—were alone in the Arctic Ocean.

For 11 months, Victoria heard not a word of "her" expedition. This was to be expected. In the age before radio, the Arctic held its secrets well.

However, on May 30, 1914, the city—and the world—was shocked by the headlines: KARLUK ICE-CRUSHED, LIES ON BOTTOM IN POLAR WATERS.

Stunned Victorians read of the stout little ship they had so gaily seen off from Esquimalt...

For five months and a day, the *Karluk* had drifted back, a prisoner of the ice. January 14, 1914, brought the end. A storm had been raging since New Year's Day and, that night, the thermometer registering 54 degrees below zero, valiant *Karluk* gave up the fight. A moaning from deep in her bowels warned that the ice had finally cracked her seams. In the eerie glow of a lamp, the sound of rushing water in his ears, Captain Bartlett gave the fateful order to abandon ship.

He had foreseen this grim eventuality and had had huts built on the ice, cramming them with supplies. As the last seaman and scientist carried his few personal effects over the side, Bartlett retired to his cabin. He knew that there was some time left before the *Karluk* slipped under; time enough for him to consider his grave responsibility. Twenty-four lives depended upon his command. Sitting in the warm cabin, home for seven long months, he played his small collection of records on the Victrola. By now, *Karluk* was rapidly settling and, as the seas hungrily reached for the upper deck, he placed Chopin's Funeral March under the needle. To the March's solemn strains, Bartlett stepped over the railing, now level with the ice.

Seconds later, the *Karluk* was gone.

Bartlett realized that their only hope lay in reaching Wrangel Island, 100 miles distant. Accordingly, he soon had his men placing caches of supplies and equipment along the intended route. The seamen were inspired to swift work by a threat more imminent than that of starvation or freezing—the icefield was breaking up underfoot. Storm and sea were cracking, shifting, smashing their icy plateau... fissures opening and closing without warning. At any instant, the marooned seamen could be swallowed without trace.

Another danger also faced them—mutiny. Even before *Karluk* had cleared Esquimalt, there had been rumblings of discontent; not only in the fo'c'sle, but among the scientists. Dr. Anderson, second-in-command of the expedition, had become openly hostile to his former friend, Stefansson. By the time he and his southern section had been delivered to their stations, Anderson's animosity towards his superior had reached the point of implacable hatred. This ill feeling had spread throughout the ship, creating several camps, each suspicious of, and antagonistic towards, the others.

With the foundering of the *Karluk,* their hostility erupted into the open.

157

Of all places, the Arctic must be the poorest to choose as political arena. Here, above all else, men must stick together. When they do not—they die.

Dr. Alister Forbes Mackay, party physician; James Murray, oceanographer; Dr. Henri Beuchat, anthropologist; and Stanley Morris, seaman, refused to follow Bartlett, blaming him for the *Karluk's* loss. It was here that the seed of tragedy became apparent, most experts agreeing that, had Stefansson not been marooned in Harrison Bay, but had been aboard the *Karluk* when she wrecked, the ship's complement would have survived without the loss of a single life. For it was Stefansson alone who really knew the Arctic. Without his experienced lead, the others, including Bartlett, would show a painful—indeed, fatal—lack of Arctic expertise.

Both Mackay and Murray had been to the Antarctic with Sir Ernest Shackleton. But their experience of the southern ice continent did them little good in Canada's frozen north. With their two companions and what provisions they could pull on a single sled, enough for 50 days, they bravely tramped away. Like Sir John Franklin's command of 65 years before, they squared their shoulders and marched into oblivion.

They did meet one of Bartlett's caching parties on the trail, the latter imploring them to return to camp. But the quartet pushed onward. Their fate, that of carbon monoxide poisoning, was not learned until 1923, when the schooner *Herman* discovered their bones on Herald Island. This find made a 1915 news clipping all the more mysterious. For, in April of that year, Eskimos reported having sighted a white man, adrift on an iceberg, the previous winter. The floe was drifting towards Wrangel Island when they tried to reach him. But a sudden wind blew his 'berg out to sea. Strangely, had he hailed them when first sighted, they could have rescued him. As it was, they had assumed him to be another native hunter. Upon returning to the village and learning that he was not, it was too late. He was believed to be a survivor of Stefansson's missing party. This mystery has not been solved since, although some have speculated that the unfortunate white man was from the wrecked whaler *New Jersey*...

Upon Mackay and company's departure, Bartlett's command had begun the terrifying march to Wrangel Island. All had to hike, the sleds being reserved for provisions—and the ship's cat, with them since Esquimalt. The only other passenger was an Eskimo baby, which rode on its mother's back. An older child hiked alongside the father.

Fighting the erratic ice every inch of the way, the exhausted survivors made a pitiful few miles each day. Each night brought the increasing threat of being swallowed by the ever-shifting, ever-yawning ice. Each night dropped to -50 degrees. Every storm set them adrift on acres-wide floes, creating the problem of reaching solid ice again.

Every portage was a nightmare. The worst ordeal was "roadbuilding." Some ice jams were so jumbled and tall that the only hope of crossing was to send a crew ahead to hack away the sharp peaks with axes.

Nineteen long days later, they reached Wrangel Island—*terra firma*. Happily, they set about building igloos and collecting driftwood. But the gaiety was short-lived. They had expected to find abundant game; they found little. No one in the outside world knew of the *Karluk's* sudden end, and Wrangel was but an unexplored dot more than 100 miles from Siberia, three times as far from Alaska. With strict rationing, they had 80 days' provisions.

Faced with this grim inevitability, Bartlett decided to strike out for Siberia for aid. The fact that it had never been done before was hardly an encouragement. Luckily for the castaways, Bartlett was at home on the sea and on the ice. He had trekked hundreds of Arctic miles with Peary, and therefore reasoned that he was the logical man to make the attempt.

By now it was March, and time was rapidly running out. If Bartlett did not start immediately, the annual thaw would trap him between the island and Siberia. With the Eskimo, Kataktovik, dogteam and sled, and seven weeks' grub, Captain Bartlett began the epic race against time.

The first 10 days, a blizzard raged without pause. When the battered Newfoundlander and Eskimo managed to reach the island's southern shore—to find themselves barred by a massive ice jam—they worked their way around this obstruction and pushed on. In the Arctic darkness, days and nights became one to the benumbed travellers; time losing all meaning. They knew only that they could not stop; that they must push on regardless how tired, how hungry, how sore they became.

One of the worst moments was the time the team broke its halter and charged ahead without the sled. The excited dogs then backtracked, the wildly gesturing Bartlett and Kataktovik terrified lest they run all the way back to Wrangel. Bartlett finally bribed their return by opening a can of pemmican as they pensively watched his slow-motion pantomime. It seemed an eternity before they approached the bait and he could grab their line.

Existing on pemmican, hardtack and tea—once, raw polar bear—they struggled ever onward. Every footstep was a battle, every mile a major victory. Days passed. Still they moved ahead; onward to Siberia and help. The most time-consuming obstruction was water. Lakes on the ice-flow—ice that often was less than an inch thick— had to be skirted. When they could not detour, they had to cross; usually on their bellies. During these precarious crossings, they were painfully aware of every creak in the glass-thin ice underneath. Then they would pull the dogs across.

Two weeks later, they were clambering over the icy hummocks of the Russian shore. Having come so far, rather than being exhausted, they gained renewed strength from the short distance remaining. Finally, after 17 bone-wearying days on the trail, they reached an Eskimo village. The friendly natives gave them fresh clothing, food, and fed and rested the dogs...

North America was appalled by Bartlett's urgent telegram to Ottawa. In his message Bartlett recounted the *Karluk's* loss and requested immediate aid for those stranded on Wrangel Island. Tragically, Bartlett's race against the clock had been too slow for many. Half of the castaways were to die before help could reach them.

The American government dispatched its revenue cutter *Bear,* Russia sent the icebreakers *Vaigach* and *Taimyr.* But rescue was not to be that easy... With Bartlett, the *Bear* proceeded to Point Barrow, where Bartlett was astonished to find Burt McConnell, one of the three men who had been marooned on the ice with Stefansson when the *Karluk* was driven away by the storm. *Karluk's* men had long given up their leader's party for dead. Yet here was McConnell, with a vivid account of their escape over the drifting ice. Like Bartlett's odyssey, they had overcome awesome odds, finally reaching safety. Not only were they safe but, in the following years, before and after Stefansson learned of his ship's fate, he managed to complete almost all of the work he had hoped to do. Although at the terrible cost of 12 lives, the expedition was, scientifically, a success.

But, before the *Bear* could make Wrangel Island, she ran out of fuel. Reluctantly, she put about. The Russian icebreakers had been recalled also, as the First World War had erupted in Europe. On Wrangel Island, the dwindling survivors waited and waited. For all they knew, Bartlett and Kataktovik had perished in the Arctic wastes and no help was coming. As, at that time, none was.

Finally, the trading schooner *King and Wing* managed to strike through to Wrangel. Aboard was Burt McConnell, who did not recognize his comrades of the *Karluk,* they were so "unkempt and emaciated." Shaggy hair hung shoulder-length, haunted faces were permanently creased by anxiety. Their clothing, in which they had lived and slept for more than seven months, was shredded. At least one survivor lost 30 pounds during the ordeal.

Of the others, one had succumbed of a shooting accident, two from nephritis, eight (including Mackay's ill-fated party) had tried making it on their own and died in the attempt.

When Anderson's southern section arrived in Seattle in September of 1916, having lost one member, the Victoria *Times* remarked of the tragic Canadian Arctic Expedition which had so confidently sailed from Esquimalt three years before:

"It is a heavy price to pay to wrest the secrets of science from the rugged face of nature in the Arctic Circle."

Chapter 26

Princess Sophia:
B.C.'s Worst Marine Disaster

"Just time to say goodbye. We are foundering."

The pathetic farewell of 343 persons was flashed through the night of October 24, 1918. Then silence.

Anxiously, the rescue boats bucking gale-swept Lynn Canal listened for more. But the *Princess Sophia* was never heard from again.

With morning came calm, but only a mast tip marked the 2,320-ton liner's grave by Vanderbilt Reef. There was not one survivor...

Although, in point of fact, the *Sophia* went down in the icy waters of Lynn Canal, Alaska, her sinking remains the greatest marine tragedy in British Columbia history; not only because of the number of lives lost, but because the disaster could have so easily been avoided. The *Princess Sophia* is considered a "British Columbia wreck" because Victoria was her homeport, she was headed for the provincial capital at the time of her foundering, and because so many of her lost company were British Columbians...

Winter struck the West Coast early and hard in 1918. Driven off course during a blinding snow-storm, the *Sophia* grounded on Vanderbilt Reef in the early hours of October 24, and stuck fast, her master, Captain F. L. Locke, a veteran of 27 years' service with Canadian Pacific, immediately radioing particulars of the mishap to his superiors of the B.C. Coast Service.

Captain Locke did not think his ship was in danger. Both he and senior CPR officials believed that the *Sophia* would float off the reef on the next high tide, expected that afternoon. The salvage steamer *Tees*, just returned from rescuing the company steamer *Princess Adelaide* from reefs at Georgina Point, prepared for immediate departure from Victoria.

Aboard the *Sophia* was one of the largest lists of passengers handled that year. Most were from the interior of Alaska, having reached Whitehorse on the last boats before river navigation closed for the winter. These travellers were southbound to "civilization" to enjoy the season in a more pleasant climate. Confident that the *Sophia* would soon float off, they whiled away the time calmly.

Both Victoria newspapers, the *Colonist* and *Times,* gave the story prominent and thorough coverage, providing latest details to a news-hungry city all too familiar with marine disasters. Victorians, many of them awaiting the arrival of relatives and friends aboard the liner, followed the news accounts closely, speculated among themselves... and waited.

CPR news releases were encouraging: "The waters of Lynn Canal are well protected and no loss of life is feared..."

When the *Sophia* failed to float off on the Thursday afternoon tide, officials said that the ship was in no immediate danger, that the *Tees* would leave for the scene, that the *Princess Alice* had sailed for the north to perform a transfer of the passengers, and that, "If the weather holds fair, there should be no difficulty in getting the *Sophia* afloat on the tides which occur early next month."

Press stories carried the first hint of tragedy when they reported that a "fresh northerly breeze" was blowing down the canal, making it impossible to effect a transfer of passengers to any of the vessels standing by. These vessels were the American ships *Cedar* and *Peterson,* the auxiliary schooner *King & Wing,* and many smaller craft; mostly fishing vessels.

CPR officials remained optimistic, although they were concerned about the disrupted passenger services, having to juggle schedules and steamers in an attempt to keep all routes operating. However, they did admit publicly that they were having difficulty making contact with the *Sophia,* but reassured a concerned public that all would work out well. They said that if the situation deteriorated the many boats at the scene would take care of all those aboard the *Sophia.*

The announcement of *Sophia's* sinking hit Victoria, home of many of the ship's officers and crew, as well as passengers, like an earthquake. People were numbed. A brief wireless message had been relayed to Victoria from Juneau, stating that, sometime during the night, the liner that had made Victoria its home port since arriving from a Scottish shipyard six years before, had sunk.

In some quarters, the news was received with disbelief, Captain J.W. Troup, manager of the B.C. Coast Steamship Service, saying, "It is hardly conceivable. I cannot believe it. He tried desperately to get official confirmation or denial from Alaska. Due to the fact that the telegraphic cable to Skagway was out of commission, the only means of communication was by wireless; never too good at best of times.

Upon hearing the initial report, many Victorians held onto the hope that those aboard had been picked up by the many rescue craft standing by. Except for the wireless report that *Sophia* was lost, Victorians knew nothing, and waited impatiently for the *Princess Alice* to reach the scene. With her powerful transmitter, she would be able to report the true situation. Finally, Captain Troup was able to learn the meagre details:

When the lighthouse tender *Cedar* received *Sophia's* message that she was sinking, about 5 o'clock Thursday, she had radioed back, "We are coming. Save your juice so you can guide us." But, in the stormy blackness, the little vessel was forced to put back and anchor until daylight. At 8:30 the following morning, she radioed Alaska that only the *Sophia's* foremast was above water.

When the storm abated, members of the rescue fleet were able to walk, at low tide, over Vanderbilt Reef where the *Sophia* had perched. The rock where the hull had rested was said to be worn as smooth as "a silver dollar" by the grinding action of the ship. Apparently, heavy gusts quartering on her stern, which was not held by the reef, swung her around, the bow acting as an axis. When the bow was blown free, she filled by the head and sank...

In the five days before *Sophia's* last sailing, more than 800 persons had reached Whitehorse and Skagway, en route to the "outside." They were disappointed to find that practically no shipping accommodation was available. However, more than 300 were able to board the Grand Trunk Paciic's *Prince Rupert,* which made a special trip north. As the *Rupert* slipped from her Skagway dock, the crowd aboard cheered their good fortune. But those standing on the pier, faced with spending the winter there, did not answer, and watched her departure. Ironically, they cheered when notified that *Princess Sophia* would make another trip. Two hundred and 58 persons boarded her...

The heartbreaking task of collecting the bodies began under the personal supervision of Alaskan Governor Riggs. More than 25 boats participated in the search. The shores lining Lynn Canal were littered with victims, many of the bodies of women and children being found in liferafts; an indication that an attempt had been made to save them first. All died of exposure.

It was learned that the passengers had refused an opportunity to be taken off before the storm, evidently preferring the warmth and comfort of the ship to the cold and barren shores of Lynn Canal. In this, the barometer had performed a cruel deception. It had been rising, indicating that the weather was to improve.

One of the more tragic incidents of the disaster concerned 17-year-old Norman Blyth. He had been hastening southward to the Shoal Bay, Victoria, bedside of his mother, who was seriously ill. He had made repeated attempts to secure transportation home, but had been unsuccessful due to the heavy bookings. Aware that his mother might not recover, he made a last, desperate effort and managed to get a berth as a steward aboard the *Sophia*.

Victoria joined Skagway, Juneau and Whitehorse in mourning. Then, still benumbed by the blow, the capital received another severe shock. Exactly one week later, headlines announced the sinking of the fisheries patrol vessel *Galiano,* which had foundered in heavy seas off the Queen Charlotte Islands. With 26 persons aboard, almost all of them from Victoria, she had sailed into oblivion.

On the night of November 11, 1918—Armistice Day—*Princess Alice* returned to Vancouver, the bodies of 157 victims of the *Princess Sophia* in hastily-constructed coffins on her decks.

Chapter 27

Mystery Of The Mary Brown

"The mystery surrounding the fate of the schooner *Mary Brown,* which sailed from Alaska for (Victoria) upwards of three months ago, and which was the object of a search by the United States revenue cutter *Wolcott* quite recently, has at last been solved..."

Thus, in March of 1894, it was reported that it was "all but certain" that the schooner, while attempting to navigate the inner passage round Graham Island in the Queen Charlottes, had been "caught in one of the storms so frequent in that locality, and all hands perished."

Initial word of the Victoria-bound vessel's suspected fate had reached the provincial capital in the form of private letters from the Skeena River. That which was addressed to George Denny reportedly gave "particulars which render it impossible to doubt the accuracy of the news..."

According to Denny's correspondent, Indians arriving by canoe from Kitkatla had reported a schooner on the rocks at the upper end of Banks Island, which is situated just below the mouth of the Skeena and separates Hecate Strait and Principe Channel. Although the hulk had been badly mauled, much of it torn away, the discoverers had been able to read part of its name: *Brown.* Holed in the bow, and dismasted, the wreck evidently had been ashore for some time. Word of its finding was made all the more sombre by mention of the fact that two boats still hung from their davits, suggesting that not all, if any, of her company had been able to escape. The intrigued natives had examined the broken craft and adjacent beaches, recovering three rifles, three watches, ammunition and some money. But there "were no signs of anyone having been around at all. It is believed that everyone belonging to the craft perished before she went on (the beach)."

Other letters confirmed the report that Indian fishermen had discovered a wreck whose name ended in *Brown* on Banks Island, that there had been no sign of survivors. In due course, Collector of Customs A.R. Milne, who doubled as Receiver of Wrecks, was officially notified by Rev. Frederick L. Stephenson, an Anglican clergyman stationed at Port Essington, of the wreck's discovery. Milne passed the word on to his counterparts in various Puget Sound ports and San Francisco, as well as Captain W.D. Roach, master of the cutter *Wolcott*.

In his letter, Stephenson described the wreck (as reported to him by the native fishermen) to be "...badly damaged...and thrown high and dry with her masts both gone. The anchor and chain are out — reasons are doubtful, whether from thumping or having been cast overboard. Three rifles or guns, 45.90 cartridges, several bags of shot, gum boots and some clothing, three watches (one gold), and some money were dug up in the sand. Boxes and pieces of boats are strewn along the beach, and a flag was found, part missing, but the name *Brown* was spelled out by one the Indians.

"Possibly you are the authority I should communicate with. My Indians are searching up and down the coast for more proof as to identify or for remains of the bodies. As yet information is scarce..."

Victoria marine men speculated that the agents of the missing *Mary Brown* (assuming the wreck to be that of the overdue schooner) would send a steamer up the coast to investigate. Any hope, however, of survivors at this late date, was admitted to be without "foundation in probability."

The missing *Mary Brown* was described as a 60-ton schooner, owned and operated by Captain Marzonia Brown, of Sand Point, Alaska. Both the *Brown* and her master were well-known in the British Columbia capital, having been frequent visitors to that port. When the schooner had sailed on her last voyage, October 3, 1893, she had had a crew of six and three passengers: James (or Edward) O'Brien, manager of the Lynd-Hough Company at Sand Point; Captain Gaffney, another company official; and an unidentified lad, said to be a relative of Captain Brown.

And such was the story — brief as it was — of the wreck of the *Mary Brown*. But, instead of simply being posted as among the many small vessels to founder along this dangerous shore, the *Mary Brown* was to achieve greater status: that of mystery ship. For, in September of 1895 — two years after she sailed into eternity — "another sensation developed" in the story with the discovery of her longboat; a discovery which prompted speculation that the *Brown's* company were not victims of shipwreck, but of murder.

According to an account in the San Francisco *Chronicle*, the wreck of the *Mary Brown* had been examined by Mrs. R.H. Hazelton, sister of one of the schooner's missing passengers. Apparently Mrs. Hazelton, moved to determine her brother's fate, had journeyed to interview Rev. Stephenson; and, ultimately, to talk him into taking her to the scene of the wreck.

Once there, she and the missionary questioned Indians who lived nearby. Among the articles which the villagers had recovered from the *Brown* was a vest — a vest which had been slashed three times by what appeared to be a knife. Despite the length of time which had passed since the schooner drove ashore, and Mrs. Hazelton's expedition, the vest yet bore traces of blood on the inside lining. Another recovered article of clothing was a coat. Like the vest it was torn and bloody. In the small of the back was something else: a bullet hole.

With a gasp, Mrs. Hazelton identified the vest as having belonged to brother James O'Brien, saying that he had been wearing it when she last saw him. The coat, with its bloodstains and bullet hole, was thought to have belonged to Captain Brown.

Not unnaturally, Mrs. Hazelton leaped to the conclusion that her brother and Captain Brown had been murdered; "either to enable the crew to gain possession of the vessel and her cargo, or (to) make room for themselves in the schooner's longboat when leaving the wreck." (This surmise was based upon the fact that the *Brown's* longboat was missing).

But it was not long before another discovery exploded both theories — and inspired a third. For the missing longboat had since been located — in good condition, at a point many miles from the wreck. This discovery, plus the information that an ex-convict named Louis Sharp, who had served two years in San Quentin for a "murderous assault" upon James O'Brien, had returned to Alaska shortly before the *Mary Brown* sailed on her final voyage, seemed to point to violence other than that of a storm.

Because the longboat had been recovered the previous winter on Montague Island, so many miles from where the *Mary Brown* crashed ashore, and it was thought to be "incredible" that it could have drifted there, authorities were faced with a tantalizing puzzle: What has become of the crew of the *Mary Brown*? Did they murder Marzovia (sic) Brown and James O'Brien, wreck the schooner and escape safely in the longboat, or did they suffer a common death with Brown and O'Brien in the wreck of the schooner by stress of weather?"

Other questions involved the schooner's cargo which, according to one report, was not found in the wreck. And, what of the *Mary Brown's* lost company? Not a single body was ever recovered. Did the fact that her longboat was recovered so far from the scene of the wreck indicate that at least some of her complement made it to shore? If so, why had they not turned up? Also, what of the mysterious Mr. Sharp, ex-convict and avowed enemy of James O'Brien? According to Mrs.

Hazelton's investigation, Louis Sharp had returned to Sand Point and been accepted as a crewman for the schooner's last voyage!

The dauntless Mrs. Hazelton, although convinced that James was dead, had vowed to solve the mystery of her brother's fate at whatever cost. But, alas, there the story ends. More than three-quarters of a century after, the mystery of the *Mary Brown* remains just that—a mystery.

Chapter 28

Miraculous Escape Of The Tatjana

"Hand over hand along a single hempen rope, with foam swirling beneath them, and huge combers clutching at their dangling, swaying bodies..."

Such was the dramatic, and dangerous, escape of the captain and crew of the Norwegian freighter *Tatjana,* in the early hours of February 26, 1924.

This exciting, and near-fatal chapter in the career of the ill-starred *Tatjana* began days before, as the Norwegian approached the exposed western shore of Vancouver Island. On her bridge, Captain Holvig peered into a grey void. With his wireless out of operation, his ship slowly proceeding by dead reckoning, he inched his way forward. Hour by hour, the *Tatjana* thumped eerily onward through the fog and rain towards the Vancouver Island coast, and, unknown to her crew, disaster.

At midnight of February 25, Captain Holvig gave the order to heave to, when he sounded. The lead line showed the freighter to be in 40 fathoms and, reassured, Holvig ordered slow ahead. Fifteen minutes later, the *Tatjana* shuddered to a stop, having crashed headlong onto the rocks of Village Island, which, but a year earlier, had claimed the steamer *Tuscan Prince.*

Seized by giant combers which roared in from hundreds of miles at sea, the *Tatjana* "lurched forward higher and higher until she came finally to rest with the jagged rocks penetrating far into her hull. So dark was it, and so thick the mist, and driving rain, that the bow of the ship could hardly be seen from the bridge..."

Instantly, Holvig ordered all hands on deck, his officers seeing to the readiness of the lifeboats. But, even as his crew ran to their stations, Holvig knew it was hopeless. No lifeboat could live in that rage of surf and rock. Almost as certain as the fate which awaited them should they attempt to reach shore by boat was that which stared them in the face if they remained aboard the *Tatjana*. For the freighter groaned with every crashing sea and seemed as though she must lift up, and off, the reef at any moment. Should she succeed in slipping free of the rocks impaling her hull, Holvig thought, she would begin to fill immediately, with the result that all 26 men aboard would be drowned when she settled beneath the combers now breaking over her stern.

Fortunately for the *Tatjana's* frightened company, there were those on board equal to the occasion: 19-year-old galley boy, and former Victorian, Garry Brown, and seaman Arthur Samsing.

When, "huddled on the foc'sil head in the mist and rain and darkness, the crew recognized that they could never succeed in launching the lifeboats in the heavy surf and that the ship might sink in deep water at any minute," it was Samsing who volunteered to secure a lifeline to a high pinnacle of rock which they could just make out, jutting from the sea, some 30 feet from the freighter's bow.

A light line was tied about the heroic seaman's ankle and he was gingerly lowered, face down, over the ship's side. Suspended in mid-air by his shipmates, his life was literally in their hands as he waited for the exact moment of "launching." Ever so slowly, and exercising every care so as not to smash him against the *Tatjana's* hull, several of the crew began to swing him, pendulum-fashion, over the waves. Back and forth, back and forth, in an ever-widening arc, he was swept over the combers breaking against the side of the ship, but a few feet below him. Almost blinded by, and choking on, the salt spray, he was swung back and forth until, "coinciding with the shoreward rush of a big comber, he was launched forward on its crest in the direction of the pinnacle of rock."

The 50-year-old record of Samsing's noble and awe-inspiring act of courage quite properly termed his successful bid to reach the "huge crag" a miracle.

However, the seaman's troubles had just begun. For, as he stabbed desperately for a handhold at the base of the pinnacle, the surf alternately smashed him against the rocks, when, upon receding, it would clutch at him with overpowering force and attempt to draw him back into its fold. Somehow—even Samsing was not sure, afterwards, how he did it—he climbed that pillar of stone. Hands bleeding, fingernails torn, he fought his way upward. His eyes were swollen shut by the biting spray, yet he refused to be beaten.

Finally—miraculously—he reached the top, and the base of a small fir which had taken root in a fissure in the stone.

By this time, his strength was rapidly failing him and, terrified lest he collapse, exhausted, before he could complete his mission, he fought to tie his line to the fir. Battered and bleeding, his fingers refused to follow his commands, and he fumbled at the line for several long, agonizing minutes before it was made fast and he was able to signal his shipmates to secure it to a heavier hawser.

Aboard the *Tatjana*, where 25 men had waited in desperation for his signal, Samsing's reassuring jerk on the lifeline brought cheers to the seamen's lips. Moments later, they had secured the first line to a second, stronger hawser, which Samsing drew to his rocky perch and made secure to the lone fir tree. That completed, he watched as his comrades prepared to abandon ship.

One by one, hand over hand, the Norwegians made their escape from the *Tatjana's* heaving decks, "with foam swirling beneath them, and huge combers clutching at their dangling, swaying bodies..." Finally all were safe on the narrow perch, separated some 30 yards from shore by a maze of rock, breaker and cross-current.

This time Samsing could not help them. Bruised and overcome by cold, he huddled on the wet rocks, a victim of exhaustion and exposure. It remained for another volunteer, young galley hand Harry Brown, to answer the call for the second, and last, leg of their flight from the *Tatjana*.

"With a light line encircling his waist," reported the *Colonist,* Brown "plunged in and battled his way some 30 yards to shore. With difficulty, so cold was he, and so benumbed his hands, he made his line fast to a rock. He could not have handled a larger rope himself, so second mate Hanson followed him to shore and secured a heavier line to the boulder. Over this the rest of the crew swung their way to the beach..."

With daylight, second engineer Sivertsen, steward Petersen and second mate Hanson reboarded the *Tatjana,* which was still lodged on the reef. Looting the ship of tarpaulins, food and kerosene with which to start a fire, they relayed the vital supplies by way of the lifeline, when those ashore made themselves as comfortable as possible. As the surf had fallen considerably, six crewmen decided to launch one of the *Tatjana's* lifeboats, and, late that afternoon, they pulled for Bamfield, to be transferred to HMCS *Armentieres* just as darkness fell. The naval patrol craft then took them back to Bamfield for the night.

The next morning, *Armentieres* proceeded to the scene of the wreck and removed the remainder of the crew, but for Captain Holvig, the first mate and chief engineer, who volunteered to stand by the wreck aboard the coastal steamer *Tees,* which also had arrived.

When asked if he knew of the wireless direction-finding stations at Pachena and Tatoosh lights, second mate Hanson replied that he had been aware of their existence, having been in these waters during the previous voyage aboard the *Tatjana,* some three months earlier. But, he explained, the Norwegian freighter had been unable to ask her

171

bearings of Pachena Point during the hours leading up to her stranding because her wireless was out of commission at the time. Not until after she hit the beach had her radio operator been able to repair her wireless and report her predicament to the rest of the world.

Because of the heroism of Brown and Samsing, the *Tatjana's* company survived without fatality. Surprisingly, their ship also escaped the Graveyard of the Pacific (one of the few vessels which came to grief here and which lived to sail again). Although abandoned as a total loss by her owners, she was pulled free by the Pacific Salvage Company, rebuilt, and returned to service under charter to the Robert Dollar Steamship Company. In July of 1925, after having completed two voyages for the American firm, it was reported that the *Tatjana* had been resold, to once more sail under the Norwegian flag.

Chapter 29

The Ship That Cried

The ship that cried: this was the ill-fated lady *Canadian Exporter,* whose seagoing career was cut short by misfortune, half a century ago.

Although but a year from her builders, the *Canadian Exporter* seems to have been doomed from the moment she docked in Vancouver Harbor, back in July of 1921. Beset by labor and mechanical difficulties, she sailed on July 29 with an inexperienced crew to load lumber at Portland for Australia.

But the Canadian Government Merchant Marine freighter never made it beyond the coast of Washington. Three days after sailing, she was reported to be aground, with a heavy list, on the sandbar at the entrance to Willapa Harbor. With three anchors out, the *Exporter* strained in the surf as the salvage tug *Algerine* hastened to her side. Upon the latter's arrival, on the morning of August 1, her master decided to wait until high water, at 10 o'clock that night, when an attempt would be made to pull the steamship free.

Although the American tug *Wallula* had made an earlier effort to tow her off without success, A.C. Burdick, manager of the Pacific Salvage Company, foresaw no difficulty as the *Algerine* was considerably more powerful than the American tug. Greatest obstacle to salvage was the fact that the *Exporter* was held, broadside, on the bar, with both bow and stern afloat, but with her soft underbelly fast aground.

Joining the *Algerine* in her day-long vigil was the U.S. Coast Guard cutter *Snohomish,* from Seattle, and several more American tugs.

Just how the *Exporter* went ashore in calm seas remained something of a mystery, although it was known to have been foggy at the time of her stranding, on Sunday, July 31. As the weather continued to hold, those on the scene remained confident that the freighter would be freed with little difficulty or serious damage.

First word of the mishap had been received by Lloyds agent E.M. Cherry, at Astoria, who relayed the message to Vancouver. Within the hour, the *Algerine* and her hastily-assembled crew steamed from port. Also aboard the large salvage tug was Captain W.H. Logan, or the London Salvage Association. Captain W.B. Finglass, assistant marine superintendent of the CGMM, boarded at Victoria after rushing from the mainland by seaplane.

Four hundred feet long, the year-old *Exporter* had been built by the Vancouver yard of Coughlin. At the time of her sailing for Portland she had aboard a part cargo of lumber.

Immediately upon her striking, it was reported, Captain William Bradley had ordered his anchors out and the pumps started to discharge her water ballast. As it was impossible to determine the full extent of her injuries in the fog, fear was expressed ashore for the safety of her company and the lifesaving crews at nearby South Bend prepared to rush to her aid until assured by Captain Bradley that she did not appear to be in immediate danger of breaking up.

At 2:30 on the morning of Tuesday, August 2, the Gordon Head wireless station received a message to the effect that the *Canadian Exporter,* despite the efforts of the *Algerine,* remained fast on Willapa Spit.

By the following day, it was official: the freighter was a total loss, having broken in two.

The disappointed *Algerine* remained alongside so as to remove whatever gear might be salvaged, but was expected to head back to port shortly. Aboard her were the *Exporter's* officers and crew, who had been evacuated without mishap.

"Since grounding early Sunday morning," reported the *Colonist,* "the ship...had been exposed to the full force of the swells coming in from the open Pacific. The ceaseless battering of the breakers had strained her badly the day before, and yesterday proved too much to be withstood longer. Hard and fast amidships as she was, with bow and stern in deep water, every comber was a blow that told severely.

"Attempts by the *Algerine* to pull her off the previous night were unsuccessful. The combined power of the salvage steamer and the cutter *Snohomish* was without avail in moving the *Exporter,* firmly embedded as she was in the sand..."

First to learn of the freighter's fate was manager Burdick of Pacific Salvage, who was informed by wireless: "Ship broken in two. Further efforts useless. Endeavoring to remove gear. Crew all safe on *Algerine.*"

The cutter *Snohomish* confirmed the *Exporter's* end and said she would transport the doomed steamer's crew to Victoria, after assisting the *Algerine* to remove her gear. That vessel reported herself to be standing by until morning. If the weather held she would make a further attempt at salvaging equipment from the wreck. If the weather deteriorated she would sail for Victoria.

When the *Algerine* did berth in the Inner Harbor, her officers and crew had an eerie story for the reporters lining the dock.

Their first view of the wreck, said T.W. Allan, superintendent of salvage, had been of the *Exporter* awash in the breakers that roared in from the open Pacific, to strike her one thundering blow after another. Groaning and sagging under the onslaught, the abandoned freighter slowly yielded, her hull parting amidships.

As the powerful tug approached the dying *Exporter* early that morning, her crew was astonished to hear a long blast from her whistle. Aware that all of her company had been evacuated, the salvors concluded that "some chance tightening of the whistle cord" was responsible. Dismissing any possibility of the supernatural, Allan, anxious that all steam remaining in the ship's boilers be saved to assist in the salvage operation, ordered a launch put over the side, recounting:

"As we drew near, we saw the reason. The ship was breaking before our very eyes. The crack appeared first in her side, just forward of the engine room, then traveled slowly down, widening as it went. The whistle cord, running back from the bridge, would become taut as the bow sagged with each passing swell, and the whistle would give a blast.

"She kept that up for an hour and a half. When she stopped she had parted in two, and a gap of three feet separated the sections. She sounded her own funeral note until no steam was left in her boilers. It was a weird experience."

By the time the *Algerine* left the scene, the *Canadian Exporter* was long silent, the three-foot split between her fore and aft sections having increased to 50. The surf continued to play with its victim, situated a mile and a half from the shore, forcing the broken halves about until the bow and stern were facing the beach, their "ragged amidships" staring forlornly out to sea.

Surrounded by a dangerous maze of sandbars and shallows, the wreck could only be approached, even by launch, at high tide. Even then it was a ticklish chore for the salvors, who had about two and a-half hours in which to remove their gear. With the falling of the tide, the area of the wreck again became one swirling eddy of breakers and undertow. Salvage operations became near disaster when one of the *Algerine's* launches was swept into the narrow gap then separating the bow and stern, its crew experiencing a harrowing struggle against the surf before pulling to safety.

Then the *Canadian Exporter* was abandoned to the sea and the underwriters, the U.S. Coastguard promising to keep an eye on the wreck so as to prevent looting by those willing to defy the breakers in quest of booty.

175

According to the *Algerine's* officers, they had been cheated by a day. Another 24 hours, said Allan, and they would have been able to tow her free. "On that outside coast," he said, "it's just a matter of time. Ships seldom get off. At any other time of the year we could never have touched her. As it was, one more day and I think we would have got her. She broke up before we had a chance to do our best."

Main reason for their failure, he thought, had been the *Exporter's* having stranded broadside on to the beach, thereby allowing the surf to swirl about both bow and stern, the resulting undertow increasing the rocking-horse effect of the sandbar under her keel. As the fore and aft sections, which were in deep water, see-sawed on the bar, the strain on her keel increased until her back broke and her fate was sealed.

The *Algerine* had made one attempt to haul her free on the high tide of Monday night, her company having been sure that, "the way in which she moved with the seas...she would come off fairly readily." But it was not to be. Despite the herculean efforts of the *Algerine* and *Snohomish,* the vessels working in tandem, with the tug astern of the cutter, they could not shift the *Exporter* more than three points.

"As the night looked threatening, and the crippled steamer was cracking and muttering as her plates began to buckle, the crew, hitherto standing by their ship," was taken off by boats from the lifesaving station at South Bend in an "efficient and expeditious manner" that earned the praise of all concerned.

Despite the worsening weather, those aboard the *Algerine* continued to make preparations for another attempt at towing her free, laying out more cables and anchors. But with morning the *Exporter* — her ghostly whistle protesting all the while — broke in two. Once the *Algerine* had recovered her gear, she headed for Victoria with 18 of the steamer's crew.

Upon the *Snohomish's* arrival in the capital with Captain Bradley, his officers and 22 crewmen, reporters questioned the former as to the circumstances leading up to the stranding. But Bradley remained silent, other than to express his appreciation for the way in which the American coastguardsmen had conducted themselves.

Many of his crewmen, upon landing, had saved no more than the clothes on their backs, and promptly signed on for the forthcoming voyage of the *Exporter's* sister ship, the *Canadian Importer,* which was due to sail from Vancouver shortly. Among the survivors landed safe and sound was the ship's cat.

Mourned Captain Finglass, assistant marine superintendent of the CGMM: "It was a great pity that such a fine ship should go to pieces so easily." Any further attempts at salvage, he said, were up to the underwriters, although he personally thought any such efforts to be hopeless.

He did not know to what extent the ship was insured, but said that her cargo, some 2,000,000 feet of lumber and 250 tons of general cargo, was fully covered.

The following day, in Montreal, the CGMM announced that the *Exporter* was, in fact, fully insured, for no less than a million dollars. Five days after, Lloyds agent Cherry at Astoria was authorized to sell ship and cargo "as she lies" to the highest bidder. The cargo, it was reported by marine men who had visited the wreck, also included shingles, automobile tires — and a "consignment of extra fine booze." The latter testimonial, it can be imagined, came from firsthand knowledge.

When the official inquiry opened in Vancouver, August 12, Captain Bradley testified that he had repeatedly warned the ship's owners that the *Exporter's* compasses were faulty. He had, he said, "written again and again...protesting against the compasses, (and) suggesting remedies that would relieve the situation, but had secured no results."

The previous February, he declared, he had written assistant superintendent Finglass "a very strong letter," advising him that if repairs were not made to the starboard compass, "it was almost inevitable something would happen." A veteran deepsea mariner, he said he had made three voyages on the *Canadian Exporter,* having commanded her since she was commissioned.

Upon sailing from Vancouver, July 29, on her final voyage, he had noticed "large deviations" in the compass as the *Exporter* approached Race Rocks in thick fog. Becoming alarmed, he was about to put about for a pilot when the weather cleared and he proceeded on his way.

Noting that the compass deviation seemed to be constant, he set his course for the Columbia River by allowing for the variation. At 12:15 a.m., Sunday, he retired to his cabin, thoroughly exhausted, as he had not slept since Thursday.

Upon awakening and going to the bridge, he asked Chief Officer Campbell, who had been on duty since 4 a.m., what course he was steering. When the officer replied, Bradley said, he had assumed that the mate had fixed his position before altering course, and went into the chartroom to see the log.

He was there when, minutes after, the *Exporter* shuddered onto Willapa Bar. He then realized that the ship was a full 10 miles off course and, at the inquiry, blamed her stranding on a combination of bad steering, an unknown tide set, and compass deviation.

The "most interesting evidence" given at the hearing (at least in the opinion of a newspaper reporter) was that of Captain Finglass, the CGMM's assistant marine superintendent at Vancouver, who admitted under questioning that the masters of all four company ships had complained of problems with their compasses, which were all of the same make. The compasses of two of the vessels, the *Canadian*

177

Prospector and the *Canadian Inventor,* had been replaced with a newer model, six months before, while that of the *Canadian Importer* was replaced immediately upon the loss of the *Canadian Exporter.* As for Captain Bradley's "strong letter" of February, he had forwarded it to the head office in Montreal after having the compass tested by another master.

Being fully satisfied with the competency of the *Exporter's* officers, he had "no theories to offer" as to the cause of her stranding.

Third Officer J.K. Saint, testifying as to the vessel's faulty steering and lack of experienced seamen for helm duty, explained that he had discovered both faults when correcting course while filling in for the chief officer, who had been ill in his cabin at the start of the voyage. He had discovered his "able seamen's" inexperience, he said, when he had ordered one of the men forward for lookout duty, that worthy inquiring as to whether that position was "at the front of the ship."

For Ss. *Canadian Exporter,* the actual cause of her grounding was academic. Broken in two and awash in the breakers on the Washington shore, she was sold as she lay for the nominal sum of $2,000 to Vancouver lumber interests who hoped to salvage the bulk of her lumber cargo before the Pacific completed its work of destruction.

Chapter 30

Brother Jonathan *Vanished*
With Almost All Aboard

Death made Victoria a regular port of call, a century ago.

August 3, 1865, the Grim Reaper once again brought grim tidings: The coastal sidewheeler *Brother Jonathan,* bound to Victoria from San Francisco, had gone down off Oregon with hundreds of men, women and children, including an undetermined number of popular Victorians.

"The intelligence received yesterday of the loss of the *Brother Jonathan,* with nearly 300 lives..." sadly reported the Victoria *Colonist,* "threw our community into a state of horror and consternation. Among the passengers it was almost safe to calculate on 50 or 60 en route for Victoria; and the painful character of the news to those who had friends on board, or at least supposed to be on board, can well be imagined.

"The few particulars which we are enabled to record of the loss of the ill-fated steamship unfortunately leaves all those who are apprehensive of having had relations or friends on board in a most heartrending state of suspense. Gladly would we, if we could, soothe each aching heart by being able to state that the loved one was not amongst the victims of the sad catastrophe, but there is no alternative left but to patiently and submissively await the receipt of further intelligence by the *Enterprise* from New Westminster this evening.

"We were beseiged yesterday with anxious enquiries respecting the names of those who were on board but the telegraph so far is painfully silent as to the names of either the lost or saved. We have learned the names of many who were supposed to be on board, but while all is here surmise it would be cruel to probe a bleeding wound and to add to the anguish of suspense by publishing names."

And so Victorians waited. Waited for seven agonizing days—a week of anguish—through one frantic delay after another in learning who had been saved...and who had not.

First reports of the calamity were painfully sketchy. Little was sure beyond the fact that the *Jonathan* had struck a reef off St. George Point, near Crescent City, Ore., in waters "well known to be a dangerous locality." Only one of the steamer's boats was known to have made shore, with its tiny crew of 14 men, a woman and a child, whose identities were unreported. Two other lifeboats, said the report, had been swamped alongside the stricken ship; nothing had been learned of the remaining three craft and their occupants, if any.

The 16 survivors had reached Crescent City, to give first word of the disaster. Infantry Capt. Thomas Buckley, of Camp Lincoln, immediately dispatched his men to the indicated beach to search for survivors and bodies. It was feared that the *Jonathan's* most prominent passenger, Brig.-Gen. George Wright was among the lost. When last seen, the stoic officer was standing on the sloping deck, a life preserver in his hands.

Hopes of those awaiting word of *Jonathan's* missing hundreds surged upward, the next day, when the *Colonist* printed a letter from William G. Young, in which he pointed out that the steamer's emergency equipment and capable officers during his passage two voyages earlier: "The vessel then carried, and I believe always carried, six if not seven, boats. Four of these were hoisted up, two immediately abaft the paddle boxes, and two on the quarters, and could be readily lowered into the water. Other two, which were metal lifeboats, were stowed bottom up on the upper deck, and with a sufficiency of hands at command and a small amount of professional knowledge, could be put in the water without any serious delay.

"These boats collectively would, I think, if the water were smooth, which it most likely was at this season of the year, hold on an emergency about 250 persons. The ship was well supplied with life preservers; they were in every cabin, and in other available positions. According to her certificate of inspection she was built at San Francisco in 1861 or 1862, I forget now which, but at all events subsequent to the date of the disaster which befell the *Commodore* in 1858, to which you allude, and when speaking to the chief officer on this subject he assured me that the vessel was to all intents and purposes a new vessel, and as staunch as any afloat, having been entirely rebuilt from her kelson upwards."

Mr. Young was in error on the latter points, the *Jonathan* having been built in 1852 as the *Commodore,* and narrowly escaping disaster six years later, with 350 persons aboard, when only the jettisoning of much of her cargo of livestock and freight had saved her. She had, however, been rebuilt as Young stated.

As for the ship herself, and her officers, Young had "no hesitation in saying that I believe the *Jonathan,* properly handled, to have been a good and safe sea boat. Her commander, Capt. DeWolfe (sic), and her chief officer, were unquestionably true sailors; ever watchful, careful and cool, and men in whom I would place every confidence in time of danger. They had both been on the coast for years, and were intimately acquainted with its navigation."

In conclusion, Young could not, "under these circumstances, believe that so many lives have been lost as reported; and, if the report of the calamity be true at all, I trust that any present impression that many more must have been saved by the boats of the vessel will prove to be not unfounded. The report says nothing of the *sinking* of the ship. Her certificate declared she was well found in pumps, and it seems to me that at present there is really nothing against the reasonable surmise that being so close to the shore she may have been run on the beach, as was the *Northerner* some years back, when comparatively few persons were drowned.

"My sole object in now addressing you is to place before you certain facts which may, I trust, be the means of soothing the public mind until further particulars are obtained of a calamity so dreadful."

Sadly, as Victorians were to soon learn, to their grief, it was all too true. The worst had happened, *Brother Jonathan* had foundered with great loss of life.

Midnight, August 4, the steamer *Enterprise* returned from New Westminster. She had been chartered by C.W. Wallace to pick up the latest dispatches but returned disappointed after having waited 33 hours. Brush fires had cut the telegraph line in Washington. *Enterprise* had succeeded in sending several queries as far as Olympia before communication was lost, but had received no replies.

A Westminster newspaper had, however, received part of a two-day-old dispatch from Seattle, which named the survivors—19, instead of the previously reported 16—forwarded by James Patterson, the *Jonathan's* third officer. Patterson ended his report with word that a rescue fleet of small craft had returned empty-handed from the wreck site. *Brother Jonathan* and her company had vanished. "We have given up all hope," he concluded.

Passing steamers had reported no signs of either the ship or of her hundreds. When communication was at last restored, two Victorians received short messages, when, just as Seattle prepared to transmit the desperately-awaited passenger list, the wires were cut again. One of the personal messages received brought joy to one Victoria family, at least. A.F. Main had wired his mother-in-law from San Francisco that he and his wife had not sailed on the *Jonathan* as feared.

Finally, the coveted passenger list arrived from Westminster aboard the steamer *Otter,* Capt. Swanson having delayed his departure for hours that he might obtain the *British Columbian* "extras." Hundreds greeted the *Otter* at the dock, when, "displaying the greatest anxiety," they stormed aboard to secure precious copies from the purser.

Among the list of 138 persons still missing and presumed lost, "appear the names of two or three families coming to Victoria under the charge of Mrs. J.C. Keenan who was herself, we fear, beyond all doubt drowned." Wife of the chief engineer of the Victoria Fire Department, Mrs. Keenan was treated less kindly by an American newspaper which described her little company of "families," as the *Colonist* termed them, "the seven soiled doves." Which paper was the more accurate, we cannot say.

Also among the missing was noted San Francisco journalist James Nisbit, thought to be en route to Victoria to satisfy a years-long desire. It was also learned that Maj. E.W. Eddy, U.S. Army Paymaster, missing with an enormous payroll, had had a premonition of disaster. He had, it was reported, balanced his books, settled his private affairs and made out his will, explaining to friends that he "felt a presentiment that he should never return." Sadly, his strange message from the nether-world proved correct.

By August 9, all telegraph lines had been repaired, but no further news had been received from the wreck scene. The next day, Victorian C.C. Beekman received a week-old telegram from Crescent City: "No more saved from the *Brother Jonathan* since our last, and no signs of the steamer whatever. Think that everything has drifted south. Have had boats out all the time up to this morning. Have given up all hopes."

Four days later, still no further word. Fires had cut the lines again.

On Aug. 16, the *Colonist* dashed all faint hope remaining for passengers and crewmen as yet unreported: "We now have sufficient to remove all hope of any other lives having been saved from the wreck."

In the same issue, readers at last learned of *Brother Jonathan's* final, terrible hours.

"On Sunday (July 30), when I took the wheel at 12 (noon)," reported the *Jonathan's* quartermaster, Jacob Yates, "it was blowing a heavy gale wind from the northwest, and we were four miles above Point St. George. The sea was running mountains high, and the ship was not making any headway. Capt. DeWolfe (sic) thought it proper to turn back, run into Crescent City, and wait until the storm ceased.

"He ordered me to put the helm hard aport, which I did, and then he told me to steady her. I did so. Her course was then due east. The time was a quarter of 1 p.m. I kept her that course until we made the Seal Rock, and then the captain ordered me to keep her southeast by south.

"It was clear where we were," continued Yates, "but smoky inshore. Then we ran along until 10 minutes of 2 o'clock p.m., when she struck the unknown sunken rock, and with such force that it felled the passengers who were standing on deck. Some of the planks started. The Captain stopped the engine and endeavored to back her off. The engineer could not get her to move an inch. She rolled about five minutes and then gave another tremendous thump on the rock when a part of her keel came up alongside; and by that time the sea and wind had slewed her around so that her head came to the wind and sea."

The *Brother Jonathan* had been mortally injured and the end came swiftly. "As soon as she came head to the sea, she worked on the rock a little; then her foremast went down through her bottom until the foreyard brought up across decks. At this time Capt. De Wolf (the first time news reports had spelled his name correctly) had been forward three times, and ordered everybody to look out for themselves, and he would do the best he could for them all."

The quartermaster was last to leave "the forward part of the ship. As I was going aft I saw a lady and gentleman standing close by the boat. I asked them why they did not get into this boat, for it was all ready to lower? They gave their heads a toss and told me they were going to get in the other boat. There was plenty of room in the boat at that time.

"As I was one of the crew of the boat, and she was being lowered, I got in her. If they had got in I would have taken my chances in another."

It had been a lucky break, indeed, for Jacob Yates. When his craft, containing 19 men, women and children, had been successfully launched, he and fellow crewmen began to row desperately for shore in the wild sea.

"As we came round the stern we saw a boat swamped which was full of women; and one boat capsized, with a man on her bottom, and also another one stove to pieces. Our boat was so full we could not take another soul in it. We would have gone to the assistance of the boatload of ladies who were swamped, but the sea was running so high and we were so heavily loaded that we could not do anything for them. I believe that if the passengers had listened to the captain and manned the boats with the ship's crew, as he wished them to do, there would have been more lives saved, for there is not a ship that sails out of San Francisco which has a better crew."

Brother Jonathan had vanished with almost all aboard in 45 terrifying minutes.

Mrs. Martha Stott, of Victoria, and her six-year-old son were among the pitifully few saved. Crewmen and male passengers had acted admirably, she said, seeing that women and children were placed in the boats first. Ironically, Capt. Samuel J. De Wolf had guided Gen. Wright's wife to another boat, saying that in which Mrs. Stott was seated was full. She had seen Mrs. Keenan in the water, wearing two life preservers. The Victoria woman had acted dazed. Someone said she had been struck by a plank or one of the boats.

"The boat was loaded down, and the passengers were obliged to bail incessantly with a bucket and a hat of one of the men. (Mrs. Stott) is positive that Yates, the quartermaster, did all in his power to get others into this boat, and says the reason so many of the crew were saved was that this being the smallest boat, the officers and gentlemen on board considered it less safe than the others, and sent the ladies in the large ones, which were lost."

Also in Mrs. Stott's boat was aged Mrs. Troudale, on her way from England to join her son in Victoria.

Another Victorian, E.J. Lonati, had been on his way home from a business trip to the Bay City, when the tragedy occurred. Fortunately, unlike so many others, his body was recovered and identified "and would doubtless receive proper Christian burial at the hands of those in authority."

Among the hundreds of grieving searchers scouring rugged Oregon beaches was Charles W. Plass; the heartbroken Napa resident was looking for his daughters Mary, her married sister and child who were journeying to Victoria to meet the husband. Despite his "every active" efforts in caring for the many dead, poor Mr. Plass saw not a trace of his own.

Several attempts have been made during the past century to recover *Brother Jonathan's* gold and silver bullion, reportedly worth the tempting sum of $350,000. But none has succeeded. The tremendous depth — 45 fathoms — defies all but the latest in salvage equipment, and exact location of the steamer's bones would be extraordinarily difficult — and expensive — to pinpoint at this late date.

Chapter 31

Secrets Kept By The Sea

Sometimes the sea chooses to yield one of her secrets; perhaps in whimsy, perhaps to maliciously taunt conceited man's ever-prying curiosity. These oddities of exotic description and questionable identity drift in with the tide onto some quiet shore. Here to lie high and dry until buried in the sands, launched again by tide and current, or found by a Sunday morning beachcomber.

Occasionally these chance discoveries are the only, haunting, clues to a forgotten tragedy. B.C.'s windswept beaches have relinquished many such grim tidings over the years.

In September, 1967, a Victoria woman found what appeared to be a message of distress at Cordova Bay. Mrs. Hugh Aylmer turned the weathered note over to Saanich police.

"Help, I am stranded at 20 degrees south latitude, 30 degrees west longitude," read the missive, written in ink on what appeared to be a "popsicle" wrapper. Corked inside a soft drink bottle by two sticks, the faded message was neither dated nor signed.

On the off-chance that it was a genuine plea for aid, officers checked the stated position, finding it to be in the vicinity of Trindada Island, a 2,000-foot-high volcanic isle 700 miles off the Brazilian coast.

As Mrs. Aylmer and police suspected, it was the work of youngsters, 13-year-old Kim Ross of Port McNeill admitting she and some friends had thrown several such "distress" messages into the sea near their northern Vancouver Island home.

Another practical joke, although of considerable more skill and imagination, had intrigued Victorians 23 years before, when Eugene Hinter and Bob Duke picked an old port wine bottle out of the sea off the Victoria Golf Club in August, 1944.

Inside was the message:

Ship *Santisuma Trinidad* burning at sea lat. 8 degrees South Long. 177 degrees West, sinking rapidly.

Under Spanish flag bound out of Fiiji (sic) to Peve, Otaherte — Fire in forward holdway kept in control for 1 day now it has spread. This hour the mizzen mast fell.

We cannot live long.

I prey (sic) the finder of this missive to inform Aherles Manville of the Admiralty, London.

I commend myself to God.

GILBERT HERN

1792

Unfortunately for lovers of the bizarre, as city detectives and naval intelligence officers were quick to point out, the pathetic note was written "in ink...on Canadian paper bearing a beaver watermark," although they conceded it definately did not sound like the work of children.

Sadly, not all notes in bottles are the creation of youngsters or impish adults. Such a pathetic farewell was found by Butedale resident, D. Cordilla, in October of 1925.

The 21-ton coaster, *Haysport No. 2,* had vanished with her four-man crew nine months before, while enroute to a northern mine with a cargo of explosives. "She was last sighted in the storm, heading out to sea. Later some wreckage was picked up, but no sign of the ship herself. None of the bodies of those on board (was) recovered."

The heartrending note simply said: "We are wrecked at Millbank Sound. No escape from drowning. Signed, Steamer *Haysport.*"

A report of another note which would seem to indicate an unknown tragedy appeared in a December, 1890, *Colonist,* under the heading, "What does it mean?"

"The following unintelligible message was found written on the back of an envelope in lead pencil, and enclosed in a small bottle, by a party of Indians walking along the shore of Clayoquot Sound, a week or so ago. It was taken to one of Mr. Charles Spring's storekeepers, and by him forwarded to this city:

August 27, 1890

Mrs. McBride, La Conner Mr. McBride, La Conner, Lillian Conner, La Conner, Alma Greenkran, Seattle.

Two Siwashes

* * *

All of Camp Delightful. One canoe missing. Don't know wheather it got through safely or not. We are sitting in the center of the pass, waiting. Amen."

What did it mean? We'll probably never know...

In many cases of shipwreck along B.C.'s jagged coast and in the stormy North Pacific, only shattered wreckage would again reach shore, grim testimony to the fate which had befallen a brave ship and her company.

Such was the loss of the British man-o-war *Condor*, which cleared Esquimalt bound for Honolulu, December 3, 1901. After conducting gunnery practice in the Strait of Juan de Fuca with HMS *Warspite*, *Condor* signalled farewell and headed for the open sea — and oblivion. Near-hurricane winds lashed the coast that night and into that maelstrom HMS *Condor* and her 104 men vanished forever.

Weeks passed before Honolulu expressed concern for the overdue warship. When the cruiser *Phaeton* search unsuccessfully, *Condor* was posted as missing...then presumed lost.

Only traces ever found of the three-masted steamer were a grating and signal book locker, which drifted up on Long Beach, and her dinghy, found by an Ahousat Indian chief. Commander D.S. Tozier, of the U.S. Coast Guard cutter *Grant,* participating in the widespread search, learned of the discovery and offered to buy the dinghy.

But the shrewd old chieftain was a hard bargainer. During the lengthy negotiations aboard the *Grant* he had spotted Tozier's dress-sword; and that was his price. When the exasperated commander saw further argument was useless, he surrendered his blade, then brought the battered dinghy to Esquimalt.

Twenty years later, a brief ceremony was held beside ailing Commander Tozier's hospital bed when he was belatedly presented a new sword by an appreciative Birtish government.

Another poignant reminder of disaster at sea is to be found in Nanaimo's historic Bastion, the old Hudson's Bay Company fort. Amid this museum's intriguing exhibits is a gold beaver, carved out of wood. Once this little figure graced the wheelhouse of the proud tug *Estelle,* which vanished with all hands off Cape Mudge, 80 years ago.

"The loss of the fine towboat *Estelle* was discussed in marine circles yesterday to the exclusion of almost all other conversations," reported the *Colonist.* "So established had been the reputation of the craft for staunchness and strength that at first the news could scarce be credited.

"It was unfortunately all too true, however, and wonder during the day gave place to genuine and sincere expressions of sympathy for those bereaved by the disaster, and speculations as to how the accident occurred. Many and wildly differing were the opinions advanced, but the majority of those familiar with the district inclined to the belief that the treacherous 'tide rip' which sets in between Cape Mudge and the mouth of the Campbell River was in some mysterious manner responsible for the catastrophe. Until further information is available — few additional particulars could be gleaned yesterday — the story of how the *Estelle* met her fate must remain untold."

Sadly, *Estelle's* sudden end remains untold to this day.

The local marine fraternity had been reluctant to believe rumors of her loss due to the fact she "was a new boat and one of the staunchest of her tonnage in Pacific waters." Built in Nanaimo but three years before, at a cost of $20,000, the 90-foot tug's boiler was just a year old.

Estelle cleared Nanaimo for northern logging camps, February 3, 1894, loaded with a cargo of chopped feed, boom chains and, according to one report, dynamite. Her crew of eight, mostly Victorians, was never seen again.

First evidence that the steamer had met with disaster came when Indians found scattered wreckage near Campbell River. Their reports were confirmed when farmer John Piercy located "two sacks of chop feed and also a life preserver" bearing her name, on the same beach.

Owner and designer of the missing tug, Andrew Haslam, MP, and Captain James Christensen, Sr., father of *Estelle's* skipper, immediately headed north on the *Brunette*. "They will this morning explore all the islands in the vicinity in the forlorn hope of picking up some survivor of the wreck, and will then report the result of their investigations, by wire, from Union (Cumberland).

"The rumor was current yesterday that the Indians on Valdez Island were witnesses of the explosion. This, however, cannot be given as authentic until confirmed by Mr. Haslam. Had the report of the steamer's destruction come from the Indians alone it would not have received much credit. But the fact of Mr. Piercy having found large fragments of the steamer, with a lifebelt bearing her name, is taken as proof positive in corroboration."

Further confirmation came when the steamer *Joan* arrived at Nanaimo from Comox to report Piercy and a neighbor named Halston had since discovered *Estelle's* shattered pilothouse and engineroom door.

Of the tug's crew, there was not a trace. Mariners could only conjecture as to her fate; recovered wreckage indicated a violent explosion. Most seafarers credited the blast to *Estelle's* having been swamped in the treacherous rips off Cape Mudge, her boiler exploding when the sea flooded over her stern. Others inclined to the belief "the explosion must have occurred through the generation of gases in the coal carried for fuel."

For many years *Estelle's* bell, recovered from the wheelhouse, called children to class at the old Quathiaski schoolhouse until the structure was razed by fire. Her gold beaver is to be seen today in Nanaimo's Bastion, as mentioned.

A haunting reminder that the sea keeps more secrets than she reveals.

About The Author

Canadian history can be awfully hard on a typewriter, as author T.W. Paterson has proven over the past 15 years. During this period, the 32-year-old writer has sold almost 1,000 magazine and newspaper articles, and nine books — and worn out two typewriters in the process.

Virtually all of these writings deal with Canadian history, much of it British Columbian, Paterson having specialized in this field since beginning his journalistic career in high school. After two years as copy boy with a Victoria newspaper, he began submitting articles to magazines (mostly American, as Canadian markets for Canadian history were few and far between). Fortunately, American readers were eager to read of Canadian outlaws, shipwrecks and tragedies, and for 17-year-old Paterson, the die was cast.

Ghost towns, historic sites and events, long forgotten tragedies and crimes again come to life through his typewriter and camera as he explored the backroads and byways of Vancouver Island, and probed yellowing records in archives and libraries. Personal interviews turned up further new leads — and more fascinating articles.

In 1972 he published his first book, a modest volume covering the more spectacular tales of lost treasure in B.C. Eight more books — ranging from shipwrecks to Canadian outlaws, battles and massacres — have followed over the past four years, as he broadened his interest to the national scene. During this period he also found time to edit two Canadian historical magazines. He also writes weekly columns for three Victoria newspapers.

Paterson has four new books planned for 1977.

Bibliography

Archives, B.C. Provincial
Archives, Public
Archives, Vancouver City
Colonist, The Daily
Department of National Defence
Department of Public Works (Ottawa)
Engineering Institute of Canada
Free Press, Comox
Gibbs, James A: *Shipwrecks of the Pacific Coast,*
  Disaster Log of Ships
Gillen, I.J.
Hanson, E.P: *Stefansson: Prophet of the North*
Higgins, D.W: *The Mystic Spring*
LeBourdais, D.M: *Stefansson: Ambassador of the North*
Lewis & Dryden: *Marine History of the Pacific Northwest*
Maritime Museum of B.C.
McCurdy, H.W: *Marine History of the Pacific Northwest*
Newell, Gordon: *Ocean Liners of the 20th Century,*
  SOS North Pacific
Nicholson, George: *Vancouver Island's West Coast, 1762-1962*
Observer, Victoria
Oregon State Library
Pickford & Black Ltd., Halifax
Province, Vancouver
Putnam, G.P: *Mariner of the North: The Life of Captain Robert*
  Bartlett
Stefansson, Vilhjalmur: *The Friendly Arctic*
Sun, Vancouver
Times, Victoria *Daily*

Index

195